PRESIDENT'S MALARIA INITIATIVE

NIGERIA

Malaria Operational Plan FY 2017

TABLE OF CONTENTS

ABBREVIATIONS and ACRONYMS

ACSM	Advocacy, communication, and social mobilization
ACT	Artemisinin-based combination therapy
AL	Artemether-lumefantrine
AMFm	Affordable Medicines Facility-malaria
ANC	Antenatal care
AS/AQ	Artesunate-amodiaquine
CDC	Centers for Disease Control and Prevention
CHAI	Clinton Health Access Initiative
CHW	Community Health Worker
CMS	Central medical stores
DDIC	Direct Delivery and Information Capture
DfID	United Kingdom Department for International Development
DHIS	District health information system
DOD	Department of Defense
DOT	Directly observed therapy
DPRS	Department of Planning, Research and Statistics
DTET	Drug therapeutic efficacy testing
EPI	Expanded Program on Immunization
EUV	End-use verification
FANC	Focused antenatal care
FMoH	Federal Ministry of Health
FSN	Foreign service national
FY	Fiscal year
Global Fund	Global Fund to Fight AIDS, Tuberculosis and Malaria
GHSA	Global Health Security Agenda
GoN	Government of Nigeria
HC3	Health Communication Capacity Collaborative
HIV/AIDS	Human Immunodeficiency Virus/Acquired Immunodeficiency Syndrome
HMIS	Health management information system
HPN	Health, Population, and Nutrition
iCCM	Integrated community case management
IEC	Information, education, communication
IAS	Injectable artesunate
IPC	Interpersonal communication
IPTp	Intermittent preventive treatment for pregnant women
IRS	Indoor residual spraying
ITN	Insecticide-treated mosquito net
LGA	Local government area
LMCU	Logistics Management Coordination Unit
LMIS	Logistics Management Information System
M&E	Monitoring and Evaluation
MAPS	Malaria Action Program for States

MIA	Malaria Implementation Assessment
MIP	Malaria in pregnancy
MNCH	Maternal, Newborn and Child Health
MoH	Ministry of Health
MOP	Malaria Operational Plan
NAFDAC	National Agency for Food and Drug Administration and Control
NDHS	Nigeria Demographic and Health Survey
NFELTP	Nigeria Field Epidemiology and Laboratory Training Program
NFM	New Funding Model
NMEP	National Malaria Elimination Program
NMIS	Nigeria Malaria Indicator Survey
NMSP	National Malaria Strategic Plan
NSTOP	National Stop Transmission of Polio
OR	Operational research
PCR	Polymerase chain reaction
PEPFAR	President's Emergency Plan for AIDS Relief
PD&L	Program Design and Learning
PHC	Primary Health Care
PMI	President's Malaria Initiative
PPMVs	Proprietary patent medicine vendors
PSM	Procurement and Supply Chain Management
QA	Quality assurance
QC	Quality control
RBM	Roll Back Malaria
RDT	Rapid diagnostic test
RIA	Rapid Impact Assessment
SBCC	Social and behavior change communication
SMC	Seasonal malaria chemoprevention
SM&E	Surveillance, monitoring, and evaluation
SMEP	State Malaria Elimination Program
SOP	Standard Operating Procedures
SP	Sulfadoxine-pyrimethamine
SuNMaP	Support for the National Malaria Program
TWG	Technical Working Group
UNFPA	United Nations Fund for Population Activities
UNICEF	United Nations Children's Fund
USAID	United States Agency for International Development
USG	United States Government
WHO	World Health Organization

I. EXECUTIVE SUMMARY

When it was launched in 2005, the goal of the President's Malaria Initiative (PMI) was to reduce malaria-related mortality by 50% across 15 high-burden countries in sub-Saharan Africa through a rapid scale-up of four proven and highly effective malaria prevention and treatment measures: insecticide-treated mosquito nets (ITNs); indoor residual spraying (IRS); accurate diagnosis and prompt treatment with artemisinin-based combination therapies (ACTs); and intermittent preventive treatment of pregnant women (IPTp). With the passage of the Tom Lantos and Henry J. Hyde Global Leadership against HIV/AIDS, Tuberculosis, and Malaria Act in 2008, PMI developed a U.S. Government Malaria Strategy for 2009–2014. This strategy included a long-term vision for malaria control in which sustained high coverage with malaria prevention and treatment interventions would progressively lead to malaria-free zones in Africa, with the ultimate goal of worldwide malaria eradication by 2040-2050. Consistent with this strategy and the increase in annual appropriations supporting PMI, four new sub-Saharan African countries and one regional program in the Greater Mekong Sub-region of Southeast Asia were added in 2011. The contributions of PMI, together with those of other partners, have led to dramatic improvements in the coverage of malaria control interventions in PMI-supported countries, and all 15 original countries have documented substantial declines in all-cause mortality rates among children less than five years of age.

In 2015, PMI launched the next six-year strategy, setting forth a bold and ambitious goal and objectives. The PMI Strategy for 2015-2020 takes into account the progress over the past decade and the new challenges that have arisen. Malaria prevention and control remains a major U.S. foreign assistance objective and PMI's Strategy fully aligns with the U.S. Government's vision of ending preventable child and maternal deaths and ending extreme poverty. It is also in line with the goals articulated in the RBM Partnership's second generation global malaria action plan, *Action and Investment to defeat Malaria (AIM) 2016-2030: for a Malaria-Free World* and World Health Organization (WHO)'s updated *Global Technical Strategy for Malaria: 2016-2030*. Under the PMI Strategy 2015-2020, the U.S. Government's goal is to work with PMI-supported countries and partners to further reduce malaria deaths and substantially decrease malaria morbidity, towards the long-term goal of elimination.

Nigeria was selected as a PMI focus country in FY 2011.

PMI began with support to three states (Cross River, Zamfara, and Nasarawa). In 2012, PMI expanded to 6 more states (Sokoto, Bauchi, Benue, Ebonyi, Oyo, and Kogi), and in 2013, added 2 more states of Akwa Ibom and Kebbi for a total of 11 states. A strategy review meeting held in April 2016 revisited the states for PMI support. States were selected based on malaria disease burden, ITN use and coverage, presence of other donors, strength of state leadership, and security. Based on these criteria, 10 states were retained and Kogi, with a malaria prevalence of 5%, was replaced with Plateau State with a malaria prevalence of 36%. Support to Kogi State will be phased out in the calendar year 2016. The projected population of the 11 states to receive PMI support in 2018 is 56.3 million. PMI provides support to all 230 local government areas

(LGAs). The Global Fund is also supporting 8 of the 11 PMI-supported states. Currently, PMI and the Global Fund assist states by supporting 60-80% of their public health facilities.

This FY 2017 Malaria Operational Plan presents a detailed implementation plan for Nigeria, based on the strategies of PMI and the National Malaria Elimination Program (NMEP). It was developed in consultation with the NMEP and with the participation of national and international partners involved in malaria prevention and control in the country. The activities that PMI is proposing to support fit in well with the National Malaria Control strategy and plan and build on investments made by PMI and other partners to improve and expand malaria-related services, including the Global Fund to Fight AIDS, Tuberculosis, and Malaria (Global Fund) malaria grants. This document briefly reviews the current status of malaria control policies and interventions in Nigeria, describes progress to date, identifies challenges and unmet needs to achieving the targets of the NMEP and PMI, and provides a description of activities that are planned with FY 2017 funding.

The proposed FY 2017 PMI budget for Nigeria is $75 million. PMI will support the following intervention areas with these funds:

Entomological monitoring and insecticide resistance management:
The Nigerian National Malaria Strategic Plan (NMSP) 2014-2020 calls for entomological surveillance to provide data that will inform vector control activities as well as targeted interventions. PMI has supported entomological monitoring since 2011 as part of a two-year IRS demonstration program in Nasarawa State. In 2013 PMI expanded entomological monitoring activities from Nasarawa to six states across all of the Nigeria's five ecological zones. The ecological zones are mangrove swamps, rain forest, Guinea-savannah, Sudan-savannah, and Sahel-savannah.. The entomological monitoring provides monthly/bimonthly data on vector density and insecticide susceptibility.

In FY 2016, PMI continued and intensified longitudinal entomological surveillance in six PMI-supported states: Sokoto, Bauchi, Nasarawa, Ebonyi, Akwa Ibom, and Oyo; indoor resting densities, pyrethrum spray catches, and light/human-baited traps were conducted in all the six sites to determine mosquito biting time and speciation.

With FY 2017 funding, PMI will continue to monitor key entomological indicators in these sites that will guide further PMI interventions in the country. Entomological data will also provide information on the effect of the interventions on vector infection rates. PMI will continue support for training and equipment procurement in order to build capacity for entomological expertise at the national, state, and local levels.

Insecticide-treated nets (ITNs):
The NMSP 2014-2020 objective is to achieve universal coverage with ITNs for the 97% of the population at-risk of malaria. Universal coverage is defined as one ITN for every two persons. PMI's goal is to support the NMEP in achieving and maintaining its targets for ITN coverage and use, especially in PMI-supported states.

PMI supports mass free ITN campaigns every three years, and strengthening continuous distribution channels that include antenatal care (ANC) and immunization clinics, schools, and community-based distributions where feasible and cost-effective. Since 2010, PMI has procured a total of 32 million ITNs for mass campaigns and continuous distribution, and distributed approximately 56 million ITNs, including over 24 million ITNs procured by other partners. From December 2013 to May 2015, the NMEP and its partners distributed 58 million ITNs through mass campaigns in 17 states, including over 15 million ITNs in the eight PMI-supported states of Sokoto, Bauchi, Nasarawa, Kebbi, Cross River, Ebonyi, Zamfara, and Benue. The states that benefited from mass free ITN campaigns last had a campaign three or more years ago.

Data from two Nigeria Malaria Indicator Surveys (NMIS) show ownership of at least one ITN in a household increased substantially from 8% in 2010 to 69% in 2015. The average number of ITNs per household doubled from 0.8 to 1.6 (2015 NMIS). Eight of the eleven PMI-supported states had higher ownership of at least one ITN per household than the national average. The percentage of the total population that slept under an ITN increased from 23% in 2010 to 37% in 2015.

With FY 2017 funds, PMI will procure approximately 8,255,722 ITNs. A total of 7,079,567 ITNs will be used to support ITN mass campaigns in Bauchi and Akwa Ibom states, and over a million ITNs will be used for continuous distribution in the 11 PMI-supported states, and to internally displaced persons. FY 2017 funds will also be used to distribute the ITNs from state warehouses to the various service delivery points, and support durability monitoring for ITNs.

Indoor residual spraying (IRS):
PMI supported a two-year IRS demonstration program in Nasarawa State from 2011 to 2013. While the NMSP 2014-2020 calls for scaling-up of IRS to cover at least 40% of areas with high malaria transmission, IRS is currently only carried out in a limited number of LGAs in some states with local funds. With FY 2017 funding, PMI will continue to build NMEP's capacity to perform environmental monitoring in areas sprayed by the states and to provide technical assistance and training on entomological and insecticide resistance monitoring.

Malaria in pregnancy (MIP):
The NMSP 2014-2020 reflects the WHO policy of providing intermittent preventive treatment for pregnant women (IPTp) at every antenatal care visit after the first trimester, with four weeks between doses, providing an ITN during the first ANC visit, and prompt appropriate management of malaria illness during pregnancy. Nigeria recently experienced an increase in IPTp uptake from 13% in 2010 to 37% in 2015 (NMIS), however, effective scale-up of IPTp continues to be a challenge in Nigeria. The factors that contribute to the low uptake of IPTp in public health facilities include missed opportunities at ANCs, restriction of non-pharmacy health workers to dispense sulphadoxine-pyrimethamine (SP) drugs, and poor quality of ANC service delivery.

To address these challenges, over the past four years, PMI has procured SP for IPTp as a part of focused antenatal care support in the 11 PMI-supported states. PMI also supported scale up of the implementation of the new WHO IPTp policy, establishment of MIP working groups at national- and state-levels, development and distribution of job aids on IPTp, and initiated the processes for addressing missed opportunities for IPTp delivery.

With FY 2017 funding, PMI will continue to support capacity building for health workers according to the MIP guidelines, advocate for states to address missed opportunities for IPTp directly observed therapy, mobilization of state domestic resources to procure SP, monitor state planned SP procurement actions, improve IPTp coverage through interpersonal communication innovations for health workers, and create demand for IPTp in the community. PMI will also support implementation of IPTp as part of health facility outreach services for focused antenatal care for three states of Kebbi, Sokoto, and Zamfara in northern Nigeria where ANC attendance is less than 25%.

Case management:
The Nigerian National Guidelines for Diagnosis and Treatment of Malaria aligns with the WHO recommendations on universal diagnostic testing and treatment with an artemisinin-based combination therapy (ACT). Since PMI began in Nigeria, case management support has been directed at the following key areas: 1) procurement and distribution of diagnostic and treatment commodities; 2) training and supervision of laboratory and clinical care personnel in accurate malaria diagnostics and appropriate treatment; 3) implementation of quality assurance (QA) systems for malaria diagnostics.

With FY 2016 funding, PMI supported the scale up of quality assured case management for malaria across the supported states working with NMEP and other donors. High priority was given to increasing diagnostic testing rates and adherence to test results as artemisinin-based combination therapy is available at most service delivery points. PMI supported case management implementation through procurement and distribution of over 6.7 million rapid diagnostic tests (RDTs) and 18 million ACTs to public health facilities and enhanced capacity of service providers in malaria parasitological diagnosis. Improving QA was a focus for PMI while strengthening quality of microscopy at secondary and tertiary facilities. PMI also supported the improvement in management of severe malaria through procurement of injectable artesunate, capacity building of senior health providers, and clinical mentoring in line with revised WHO treatment guidelines.

In FY 2017, PMI will build on the progress to date and will continue to support the NMEP's malaria case management policy through provision of malaria commodities, case management training/refresher training, supportive supervision, and diagnostic quality assurance/quality control (QA/QC). PMI will procure and distribute approximately 16.5 million RDTs and 3 million ACTs to help meet the projected need in PMI supported states. PMI will plan to gradually expand the private sector activities that began as a pilot in Ebonyi with proprietary patent medicine vendors (PPMVs). Also, PMI plans to add support to seasonal malaria chemoprevention (SMC) efforts targeted at children under the age of five years in PMI-supported states in the Sahel region.

Health systems strengthening and capacity building:
PMI supports a broad array of health system strengthening activities that cut across case management; procurement and supply management; surveillance, monitoring and evaluation (SM&E); and integrated vector management.

With FY 2017 funds, PMI will work with other development partners to strengthen capacities at national and state level in effective program management. PMI funds will also be used to strengthen the capacity of facility and operational level staff in malaria case management; prevention of MIP; entomological monitoring; and SM&E. In addition, PMI will continue to provide support for the Nigeria Field Epidemiology and Laboratory Training Program (NFELTP) that builds capacity of health workers in epidemiology and disease outbreak investigations.

Social and behavior change communication (SBCC):
Nigeria's Advocacy, Communication, and Social Mobilization (ACSM) guidelines for malaria recommend various channels of communication based on the target audiences. Malaria educational messages generally reach households using radio, community drama, printed materials, community and religious leaders, and through community support groups and household visits of volunteers. Nationwide surveys have shown that there is widespread knowledge of malaria interventions however there are misconceptions about the cause and ways to manage malaria. Since 2011, PMI has provided support for SBCC across all key malaria interventions.

With FY 2017 funds, PMI will support an overarching national 'malaria-free' communications campaign to increase general awareness and use of malaria control interventions at national, state and local levels. State and local government-level activities will focus on transmitting malaria communication messages in local languages through radio, and use of community volunteers for information dissemination. Emphasis will also be placed on implementing SBCC interventions to target health care workers in order to increase compliance to malaria prevention and treatment guidelines, and improve interpersonal communication of health workers.

Surveillance, monitoring and evaluation:
Surveillance, monitoring, and evaluation (SM&E) is an integral part of the NMSP 2014-2020, with one of the primary objectives focusing on routine collection and reporting of malaria data, and use of such data for program improvement. Evidence-based decision making requires a strong and functional SM&E system that provides good quality data. PMI supports strengthening the routine health information system at various levels. Periodic population-based surveys such as the Malaria Indicator Survey (2015 NMIS) and facility-based surveys can be used to measure the status of key malaria indicators.

In the past year, PMI has continued the support for the health management information system (HMIS) strengthening at national and state levels that has led to significant improvement in completeness and timeliness of routine data reported in the PMI-supported states. With funding from PMI and partners, the National Bureau of Statistics implemented the 2015 NMIS from October 2015 through November 2015. The preliminary results were made available in March 2016, and the final analyses are expected in September 2016. The country as a whole did see a marked decrease in malaria prevalence measured by microscopy in children age 6-59 months (42% in 2010; 27% in 2015; relative difference of 36%). The end-use verification surveys are done every six months to assess stock availability of malaria commodities, testing for malaria before treatment, prescription of ACTs, storage conditions for commodities, and training of health workers.

With FY 2017 funds, PMI/Nigeria's SM&E activities will continue to rely on a combination of routine malaria data collected through the HMIS and the logistics management information system (LMIS), household surveys, health facility surveys and assessments, and information from partners. PMI will continue to strengthen the routine malaria information system at the health facility, LGA, state, and national levels through the harmonized HMIS (using the District Health Information System version 2 [DHIS2] application). PMI will help fund the next Nigeria Demographic and Health Survey (NDHS) scheduled for 2018, 10 years after the 2008 NDHS. There will be an increased focus on data analysis through triangulation, mapping, and targeting interventions based on the results of data analysis.

Operational research (OR):
The 2012 Malaria Program Review (MPR) identified a lack of OR available to inform both scientific and communications-related strategy development. The NMSP 2014-2020 proposed earmarking funding from the NMEP monitoring and evaluation (M&E) budget to OR. In 2014, the NMEP and development partners held a scientific meeting to identify priority areas in the core interventions. PMI will work with NMEP and other development partners to analyze 2015 NMIS data, and revisit the NMEP OR prioritized list to identify areas for support.

II. STRATEGY

1. Introduction

When it was launched in 2005, the goal of PMI was to reduce malaria-related mortality by 50% across 15 high-burden countries in sub-Saharan Africa through a rapid scale-up of four proven and highly effective malaria prevention and treatment measures: insecticide-treated mosquito nets (ITNs); indoor residual spraying (IRS); accurate diagnosis and prompt treatment with artemisinin-based combination therapies (ACTs); and intermittent preventive treatment of pregnant women (IPTp). With the passage of the Tom Lantos and Henry J. Hyde Global Leadership against HIV/AIDS, Tuberculosis, and Malaria Act in 2008, PMI developed a U.S. Government Malaria Strategy for 2009–2014. This strategy included a long-term vision for malaria control in which sustained high coverage with malaria prevention and treatment interventions would progressively lead to malaria-free zones in Africa, with the ultimate goal of worldwide malaria eradication by 2040-2050. Consistent with this strategy and the increase in annual appropriations supporting PMI, four new sub-Saharan African countries and one regional program in the Greater Mekong Sub-region of Southeast Asia were added in 2011. Nigeria was selected as a PMI focus country in FY 2011. The contributions of PMI, together with those of other partners, have led to dramatic improvements in the coverage of malaria control interventions in PMI-supported countries, and all 15 original countries have documented substantial declines in all-cause mortality rates among children less than five years of age.

In 2015, PMI launched the next six-year strategy, setting forth a bold and ambitious goal and objectives. The PMI Strategy for 2015-2020 takes into account the progress over the past decade and the new challenges that have arisen. Malaria prevention and control remains a major U.S. foreign assistance objective and PMI's Strategy fully aligns with the U.S. Government's vision of ending preventable child and maternal deaths and ending extreme poverty. It is also in line with the goals articulated in the RBM partnership's second generation global malaria action plan, *Action and Investment to defeat Malaria (AIM) 2016-2030: for a Malaria-Free World* and WHO's *Global Technical Strategy for Malaria, 2016-2030*. Under the PMI Strategy 2015-2020, the U.S. Government's goal is to work with PMI-supported countries and partners to further reduce malaria deaths and substantially decrease malaria morbidity, towards the long-term goal of elimination.

This FY 2017 Malaria Operational Plan presents an implementation plan for Nigeria, based on the strategies of PMI and the National Malaria Elimination Program (NMEP). It was developed in consultation with the NMEP and with the participation of national and international partners involved in malaria prevention and control in the country. The activities that PMI is proposing to support fit in well with the National Malaria Control Strategy and Plan (NMSP) and build on investments made by PMI and other partners to improve and expand malaria-related services, including the Global Fund to Fight AIDS, Tuberculosis, and Malaria (Global Fund) malaria grants. This document briefly reviews the current status of malaria control policies and interventions in Nigeria, describes progress to date, identifies challenges and unmet needs to achieving the targets of the NMEP and PMI, and provides a description of activities that are planned with FY 2017 funding.

2. Malaria situation in Nigeria

Nigeria is the most populous country in Africa with a projected total population of approximately 205 million for 2018 and an estimated annual growth rate of about 3.2%. It comprises six geopolitical zones (North West, North East, North Central, South West, South South, and South East), 36 states (plus the Federal Capital Territory of Abuja), 774 local government areas (LGAs) with an average population of about 265,793 residents per LGA, and 8,812 wards. Each state has an elected governor, an executive council, and a house of assembly with the power to enact state laws. State governments have substantial autonomy and exercise considerable authority over the allocation and utilization of their resources, limiting the influence of the federal government over state and local government affairs.

Nigeria is ranked 152 out of 188 countries in the 2015 United Nations Development Program Human Development Index. The 2015 ranking represents a two-point positive change since the 2009 ranking. Under-five mortality is estimated at 128 per 1,000 live births and maternal mortality is estimated at 576 per 100,000 live births according to 2013 Nigeria Demographic and Health Survey (DHS). Nearly all health and socioeconomic indicators in the south of the country are significantly better than in the north. For example, under-five mortality rates are about one and a half times higher and maternal mortality rates are three times higher in some northern zones than in the rest of the country. The South West Zone has the lowest under-five mortality. The country's gross domestic product increased during the past decade, with oil revenues as the main driver of the economy. However, falling oil and gas prices in the world market is affecting the Nigeria economy and the local currency, the Naira, has come under severe pressure recently, which is linked to the decrease in supply of petrodollars. Overall, economic growth of the past decade has not improved the welfare of the majority of the population nor has it affected the high incidence of poverty.

Malaria is transmitted throughout Nigeria, with 97% of the population at risk. Five ecological zones define the intensity and seasonality of transmission and mosquito vector species: mangrove swamps, rain forest, Guinea-savannah, Sudan-savannah, and Sahel-savannah. These various ecological zones with mosaics are distinguished by rainfall and other climatic conditions. The rainfall duration ranges from about three months in the Sahel-savannah to nine months in the Mangrove forest. These climatic patterns affect vegetation and most flora and fauna are differentiated across the ecological zones.

The National Malaria Strategic plan recommends at least two sentinel sites per ecological zone that will generate data on the vector bionomics and insecticide susceptibility. The duration of the transmission season ranges from year-round transmission in the south to three months or less in the north. *Plasmodium falciparum* is the predominant malaria species. The primary vector across most of the country is *An. gambiae* s.s. The data from the 2015 Nigeria Entomology Report showed that *Anopheles gambiae* s.s. was the predominant member of the *Anopheles gambiae* complex representing 78 to 100% of the population at the different sites. *Anopheles arabiensis* was the other member of the complex identified by PCR but absent in Enugu and Rivers sentinel sites. Overall, 85.7% of mosquitoes that were PCR positive were *An. gambiae* s.s. while *An. arabiensis* represented 14.3%

According to the WHO World Malaria Report 2015, there is high transmission of malaria in Nigeria with more than 76% of the population reporting more than 1 case per 1,000 population. There was a less than 50% decrease in projected incidence of malaria from 2000 – 2015. Nigeria and the Democratic Republic of Congo account for more than 35% of the global total of estimated malaria deaths. The Verbal Autopsy/Social Autopsy (VASA) Survey[1] conducted in 2014 reported that malaria, diarrheal disease, and pneumonia are the leading causes of deaths among children ages 1 – 59 months. With a major symptom of malaria being fever, the prevalence of fever care seeking serves as a proxy for malaria care seeking behavior. The 2015 Nigeria Malaria Indicator Survey (MIS) reported a fever prevalence of 41 percent in children in the last two weeks before the survey. Of those with fever, 66% sought advice or treatment and only 30% went to the public sector.

Microscopy data from the 2015 NMIS show that the prevalence of malaria in children under five years of age is 27%, with wide regional differences (Figure 1). Parasite prevalence ranges from 14% in the South East Zone to 37% in the North West Zone. The prevalence of malaria in rural population is three times that in urban populations (12% vs. 36%) and when compared to the highest socioeconomic group, the prevalence of the lowest socioeconomic group is 10 times higher (4% vs. 43%).

---

[1] National Population Commission (Nigeria), Federal Ministry of Health of Nigeria, National Bureau of Statistics (Nigeria), and Institute for International Programs at Johns Hopkins Bloomberg School of Public Health. A verbal/social autopsy study to improve estimates of the causes and determinants of neonatal and child mortality in Nigeria, 2014. Abuja, Nigeria, and Baltimore, Maryland, USA. 2016.

Figure 1: Map of Malaria Prevalence in Children 6 to 59 Months by Microscopy, 2015 NMIS

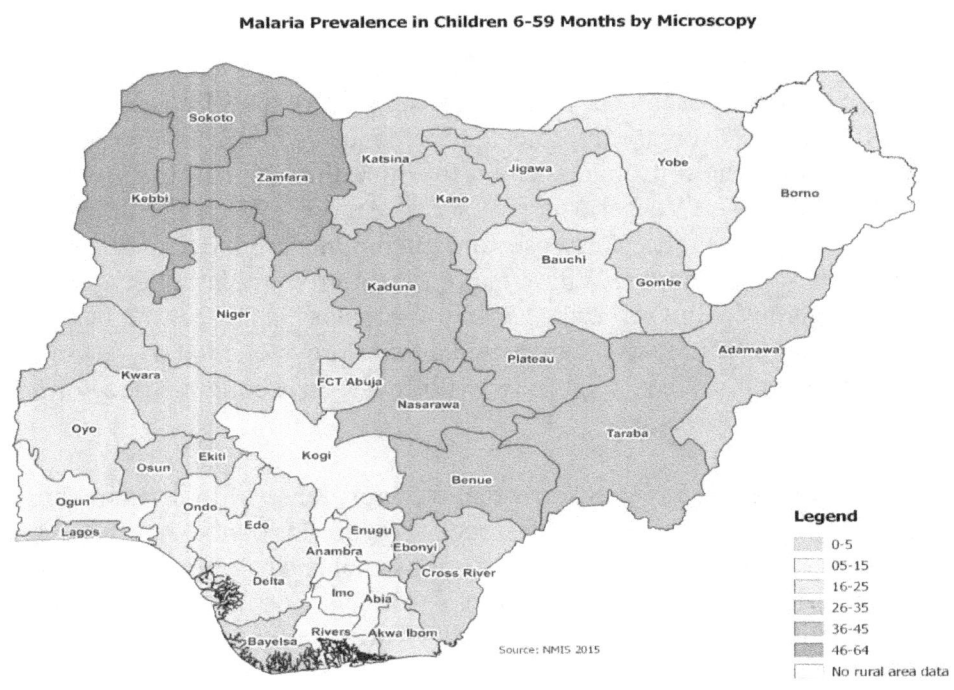

Malaria Prevalence in Children 6-59 Months by Microscopy

Source: NMIS 2015

Legend
- 0-5
- 05-15
- 16-25
- 26-35
- 36-45
- 46-64
- No rural area data

3. Country health system delivery structure and Ministry of Health organization

The public health care system is divided into three tiers, each associated with one of the administrative levels of government: federal, state, and LGA. While the 774 LGAs are the constitutionally-designated providers of primary health care, they are the weakest level of the health care system. In addition to the Federal Ministry of Health (FMoH), the National Primary Health Care Development Agency, a centrally-funded agency, has the mandate to support the promotion and implementation of high-quality and sustainable primary health care. This agency is particularly active in the development of community-based systems and functional infrastructure as well as ensuring that infants are fully immunized against vaccine-preventable diseases. The federal health budget covers tertiary care and disease control programs, including malaria control; state health budgets pay for secondary care; and LGA budgets cover primary health care. The amount of government spending on health and malaria is difficult to determine, as funding levels vary and actual spending does not always match the original budget. National Health Accounts have been developed but available reports are out of date. It is generally believed that the government spends less than 5% of its national budget on health. In 2014, the National Health Act was signed into law. The National Health Act establishes a Basic Health

Care Fund to be financed from a Federal Government Annual Grant of not less than one percent of its Consolidated Revenue Fund, supplemented by grants by international donor partners, and funds from any other source. It provides a framework for the regulation, development, and management of a national health system and sets standards for rendering health services in the federation.

Nigeria has a total of 34,173 health facilities: 30,098 primary, 3,992 secondary, and 83 tertiary. The private sector constitutes 33% of all health facilities in Nigeria. Private health facilities include private not-for-profit, private for-profit, pharmacies, proprietary patent medicine vendors (PPMVs), and mobile clinics.

Nigeria's public health system challenges include:

- Inadequate, inaccessible, and poor quality service delivery, particularly at the periphery, where most primary health care facilities offer only a limited package of services due to limited availability of trained health workers;
- Lack of necessary referral linkages between the different levels of health care;
- Weak logistics systems for commodities, with as many as six separate vertical commodities management systems with little or no coordination between them;
- Poorly maintained infrastructure with many buildings and equipment in need of repair and/or maintenance; and
- Weak institutional capacity with inadequate supervision of health services.
- Limited availability of health workers, and poor deployment in the rural health facilities.

Led by a coordinator, the NMEP consists of about 120 staff members and is divided into six branches: Program Management; Procurement and Supply Management; Integrated Vector Management; Case Management; Surveillance, Monitoring and Evaluation; and Advocacy, Communication, and Social Mobilization (ACSM). At the national level, the NMEP is responsible for establishing policies, guidelines, and norms. Each state and LGA has a Malaria Program Officer (a local civil servant) who oversees malaria activities in his or her area.

The private health care system provides care for a substantial proportion of the Nigerian population. It consists of tertiary, secondary, and primary health care facilities, as well as pharmacies, PPMVs, and unregistered drug sellers. Approximately 76% of all secondary facilities and about 28% of primary health care facilities are private. Forty-two percent of all fever cases seek treatment first in the private sector (2013 NDHS). Services provided by the private sector may be subsidized, as in missionary health facilities, or full-cost, as in privately owned clinics and hospitals. The latter are more common in urban areas. In rural areas, about two-thirds of the population lives within five kilometers of a primary health care clinic. The estimated 34,173 health facilities nationwide are fairly evenly distributed between urban and rural areas.

The total number of public health facilities in the 11 PMI-supported states is 9,788, of which PMI has supported 3,722 facilities (38%). Of the 3,722 health facilities, 3,169 (85%) receive a full package of interventions that includes ITNs; MIP; malaria case management; malaria commodities; and surveillance, monitoring, and evaluation (SM&E). The remaining 553 facilities receive only commodities that are procured by the Government of Nigeria (GoN) and other donors, which are distributed with PMI funds.

All health facilities in Nigeria receive support from the states and LGAs. PMI support for states, LGAs, and facilities is intended to fill critical gaps without becoming a substitute for resources from the government of Nigeria. The focus and level of funding of PMI support in each state are guided by the availability of other donors, and the capacity of the state and national governments to provide resources for malaria. Within each state, PMI works closely with the state and other partners to assess needs and set priorities. The needs and priorities will vary from state to state. Typically, when PMI initially partners with a state, the intervention focus is on high volume facilities in each LGA. As PMI becomes established, efforts are expanded to next level facilities in coordination with the state and partners. Overall, PMI support has expanded from 705 health facilities in 2010-2011 to 3,722 by May 2016. This expansion reflects the critical gaps expressed by NMEP and the state malaria elimination programs during joint planning meetings, and the availability of PMI resources to meet those needs.

4. National malaria control strategy

The National Malaria Strategic Plan 2014-2020 (NMSP 2014-2020) is based on the National Strategic Health Development Plan 2010-2015 and aligns with national health and development priorities. The strategy outlines the provision of a comprehensive package of integrated malaria prevention and treatment services through the community, primary, secondary, and tertiary levels. The strategy also defines the roles of each health care cadre/level relative to malaria control and case management across all health care services including public, private, and traditional health providers.

With the vision of achieving a malaria-free Nigeria and the goal of reducing malaria burden to pre-elimination levels and bringing malaria-related mortality to zero, the objectives of the NMSP 2014-2020 are to:

- Provide a least 80% of targeted populations with appropriate preventive measures by 2020
- Test all care-seeking persons with suspected malaria using RDTs or microscopy by 2020
- Treat all individuals with confirmed malaria seen in public or private facilities with effective antimalarial drugs by 2020
- Provide adequate information to all Nigerians such that at least 80% of the population habitually takes appropriate malaria preventive and treatment measures as necessary by 2020

- Ensure the timely availability of appropriate antimalarial medicines and commodities required for prevention and treatment of malaria in Nigeria wherever they are needed by 2018
- Ensure at least 80% of health facilities in all LGAs report routinely on malaria by 2020, progress is measured, and evidence is used for program improvement

Under the strategic plan, the GoN supports the provision of ITNs, IRS, larval source management, IPTp, and diagnosis and treatment of uncomplicated and severe malaria.

The NMSP 2014-2020 emphasizes the strengthening of public-private partnerships across intervention areas. Of note are the planned collaborations with corporate organizations in the conduct of IRS, implementation of IPTp, and the integration of the commodity logistics system. Perhaps most importantly however, is the recent change in elective government at federal and state levels that has brought a renewed energy for increasing national resources for health care provision.

5. Updates in the strategy section

USAID/Nigeria has developed a different operational strategy aimed to increase state ownership and sustainability of U.S. Government (USG)-funded activities. This strategy requires states to commit more resources to activities through advocacy and domestic financing. A memorandum of understanding (MOU) will guide USAID engagement with states. USAID/Nigeria and each state will have defined responsibilities and levels of support specified by the MOU. The MOUs for PMI-supported states will be in place by mid-2017.

USAID/Nigeria will use two indicators to monitor state performance: 1) proportion of the state budget allocated to health activities; and, 2) proportion of state health budget that is released to support health activities. These two indicators will be disaggregated by health account—malaria, maternal, newborn and child health (MNCH), family planning (FP), and nutrition. USAID/Nigeria could withdraw its resources from a state, should the state not meet its MOU commitments. However, any such decision will also be based on intervention coverage and epidemiologic factors to avoid leaving vulnerable populations at risk.

PMI coverage

PMI began in 2011 with support to three states (Cross River, Zamfara, and Nasarawa). In 2012, PMI expanded to 6 more states (Sokoto, Bauchi, Benue, Ebonyi, Oyo, and Kogi), and in 2013 added 2 more states, for a total of 11 states (Akwa Ibom and Kebbi). Table 1 provides a detailed description of PMI investment area for the current and future 11 PMI focus states.

A strategy review meeting held in April 2016 revisited the states that should benefit from PMI support starting with FY 2016 funds. The state selection process was guided by a tool developed by PMI that uses multiple criteria including malaria disease burden, ITN coverage, presence of other donors, complementarity of other health and USG investment, the strength of state leadership and security situation. The strategy development team recommended Nigeria to remain active in 11 states, but replace Kogi with Plateau. Kogi State was dropped because of evidence from the 2015 NMIS that showed a low malaria disease burden in the state. Both Kogi and Plateau have the same projected 2016 population of approximately 4.4 million people but malaria prevalence in Plateau in children under the age of five is 35.8% while in Kogi it is 5.4%. Kogi State is benefiting from funding from the Global Fund but Plateau has no other donor support (Figure 2).

Table 1: PMI Focus States by Start-up Year and Intervention Support as of June 2016

No.	State	Population (2017 projection)	Start-up year	ITNs	MIP/ IPTp	CM[1]	iCCM	EM[2]	BCC	Other Partners
1	Cross River	3,974,499	2011	X	X	X			X	Global Fund
2	Nasarawa	2,591,756	2011	X	X	X		X	X	
3	Zamfara	4,635,203	2011	X	X	X			X	Global Fund
4	Bauchi	6,797,416	2012	X	X	X	X	X	X	Global Fund
5	Sokoto	5,142,408	2012	X	X	X		X	X	Global Fund
6	Benue	5,868,834	2012	X	X	X			X	Global Fund
7	Ebonyi	2,957,485	2012	X	X	X	X	X	X	
8	Oyo	8,127,582	2012	X	X	X		X	X	Global Fund
9	Kogi*	4,560,271	2012	X	X	X			X	Global Fund
10	Akwa Ibom	5,698,168	2013	X	X	X		X	X	Global Fund
11	Kebbi[3]	4,554,655	2013	X	X	X			X	Global Fund
12	Plateau*	4,410,230	2017	X	X	X			X	

[1] CM=Case management
[2] EM= entomological monitoring
[3] UNICEF is supporting iCCM in Kebbi State with funding from the Gates Foundation.
*PMI support for Kogi State will end in calendar year 2016 and support for Plateau State will start in calendar year 2017.

PMI has started with Kogi State on the phase out plan. The support to Kogi State will end in calendar year 2016. The ITN free mass campaign is planned to take place in October 2016. Kogi will also receive malaria commodities (ACTs, RDTs, SP, injectable artesunate) through December 2016. The last distribution will take place in December 2016 and Kogi will receive a six month supply. After December 2016, PMI will not provide any other support to Kogi State however Kogi will continue to receive support from the Global Fund and state domestic resources.

PMI support for Plateau State will start in calendar year 2017 with FY 2016 funds. The activities will start with the state's expression of interest to partner with U.S. Government, followed by a situation analysis, to be conducted by an existing PMI implementing partner. The situation analysis findings will inform the development of the memorandum of understanding with the state. Activities will commence during the first quarter of calendar year 2017, starting with: 1) establishing an office in Plateau state; 2) development of a state malaria operational plan; 3) identification of high volume public health facilities to receive PMI support in the initial phase; 4) training of health workers in case management, MIP, HMIS, ITNs, and supply chain and logistics management as necessary; 5) distribution of malaria commodities; and 6) capacity building for SM&E and supportive supervision.

PMI overlaps with the Global Fund in 8 of the 11 states (Figure 2). With the addition of Plateau, the projected population for 2018 in the 11 PMI-supported states is 56.3 million.

Figure 2: PMI and Global Fund Supported States in 2016

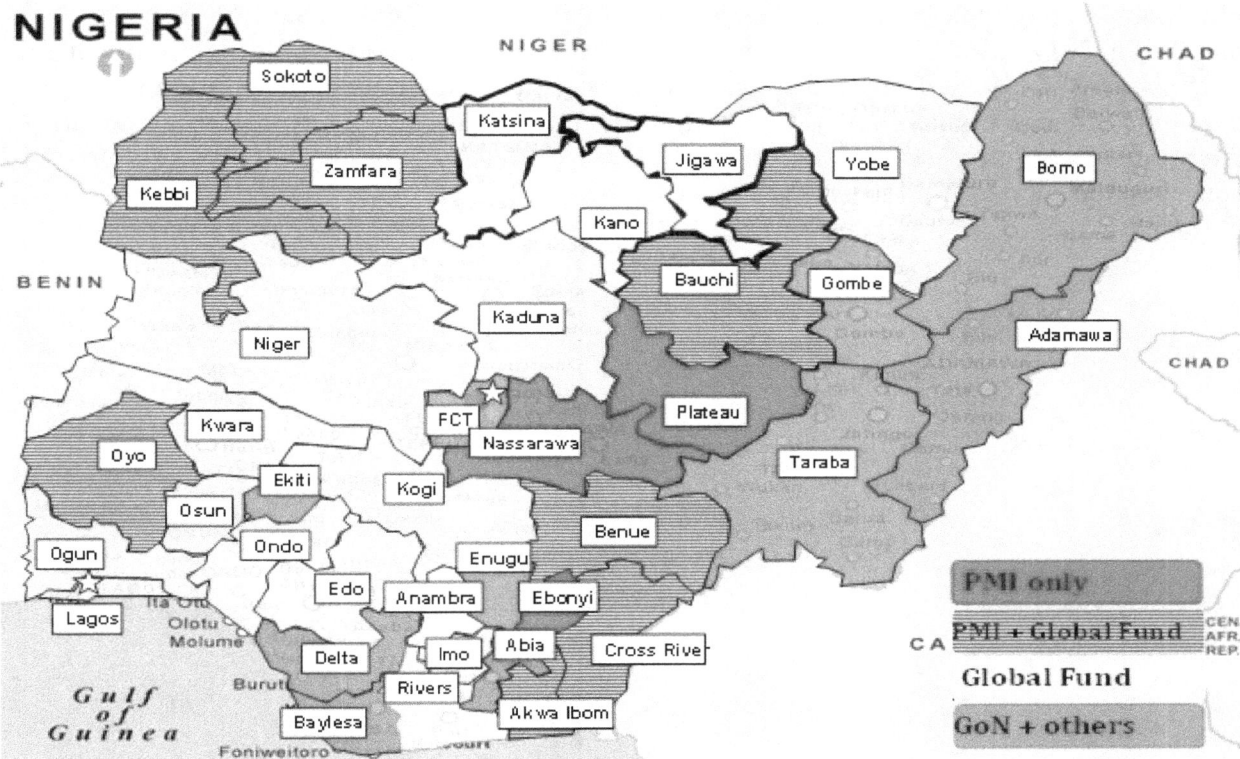

PMI currently provides support to all 230 LGAs and an average of 35-40% of health facilities per state. PMI has gradually scaled up the number of health facilities supported over time: 705 in 2010/2011; 1,441 in 2012/2013; 1 893 in 2014; 3,066 in 2015, and 3,722 by May 2016. The expansion prioritizes health facilities that operate on a daily basis, that have health workers available to provide health services (including malaria diagnosis and treatment), and that report high outpatient and/or ANC attendance. PMI support goes to a select number of health facilities within the supported LGAs. Other health facilities within the same LGAs are supported by the Global Fund, the states, and other donors.

The main sources of funding for malaria efforts within the 11 PMI-supported states are PMI, the Global Fund, and domestic resources from the states themselves. However, available external funding does not cover all technical assistance and implementation support needs for all health facilities within these 11 states. In 8 of the 11 states, the Global Fund is also supporting some 17 health facilities per LGA, leaving a significant number of health facilities unsupported by PMI or the Global Fund. On average, PMI and the Global Fund support approximately 60-80% of all health facilities in a state with commodities and technical assistance for training and supervision. Using domestic resources, the states also cover approximately an additional 10% of health facilities with malaria commodities as well as health worker salary and facility operational support more broadly.

PMI, coordinating with NMEP and other partners, will support approximately 5,000 health facilities in 2017 with FY 2016 funding, and support over 6,000 health facilities in 2018 with FY 2017 funding (Table 2). The scale-up plan addresses both the addition of more health facilities over time and also an intention to strengthen the quality of service delivery at each supported facility. The scale-up package is not standard across states or facilities because it takes into consideration support from the states and the Global Fund.

Table 2: Health Facility Scale-up plan in PMI Focus States: 2010-2018

No.	State	Total LGAs	Total HFs	Total public HFs	2010-2011 Supported HFs		2012-2013 Supported HFs		2014 Supported HFs		2015 Supported HFs		2016 Supported HFs		Proj
					Total	%	Total	%	Total	%	Total	%	Total	%	Tot
1	Akwa Ibom	31	534	452	0	0%	0	0%	452	100%	461	102%	470	104%	45
2	Bauchi	20	1,091	1,015	0	0%	415	41%	415	41%	165	16%	210	21%	62
3	Benue	23	1,284	1,034	92	9%	184	18%	184	18%	247	24%	304	29%	64
4	Cross River	18	923	774	72	9%	144	19%	144	19%	235	30%	386	50%	54
5	Ebonyi	13	594	491	56	11%	104	21%	104	21%	163	33%	372	76%	30
6	Kebbi	21	738	628	0	0%	0	0%	0	0%	165	26%	305	49%	45
7	Kogi	21	1,045	781	84	11%	84	11%	84	11%	166	21%	290	37%	0
8	Nasarawa	13	935	746	52	7%	105	14%	105	14%	186	25%	518	69%	48
9	Oyo	33	1,217	601	132	22%	132	22%	132	22%	176	29%	183	30%	45
10	Plateau	17	1,064	978	0	0%	0	0%	0	0%	0	0%	0	0%	40
11	Sokoto	23	746	715	161	23%	161	23%	161	23%	161	23%	322	45%	38
12	Zamfara	14	681	666	56	8%	112	17%	112	17%	130	20%	170	26%	37
	TOTAL	230	9,788	7,873	705	9%	1,441	18%	1,893	24%	2,255	28.6%	3,530	45%	5,0

Notes:

- PMI support for Kogi state will end in calendar year 2016
- PMI support for Plateau state will commence in calendar year 2017
- The Global Fund and PMI co-exist in eight of the 11 PMI focus states (GF is not working in Ebonyi, Nasarawa, and Plateau states).
- The Global Fund supports a17 health facilities in each LGA
- An additional 553 health facilities received commodities procured by the GoN and other donors and distributed with PMI funds in 2015 and 2016

Table 3 provides an illustration of PMI scale-up plan for capacity building activities for malaria case management and MIP.

Table 3: Scale-up Training Plan of Health workers in Case Management and MIP

Fiscal Year	No. of HWs Trained on MIP	Case Management	
		No. of HWs Trained on ACT use	No of HWs Trained on RDT use
2011	No data	No data	No data
2012	3,456	5,608	3,555
2013	1,466	24,195	1,919
2014	1,630	14,923	1,629
2015	3,098	6,866	2,262
2016 (Target)	1,149	1,414	1,713
2017 (Projected)	2,500	5,000	5,000
2018 (Projected)	2,500	5,000	5,000
Total Trained with PMI Funds	15,799	63,006	21,078
Eligible health workers (Health Facility and Community)	42,128	116,033	116,033
Total Coverage (Percent)	38%	54%	18%

Note:
- Training data for 2014-2016 is for the 11 states
- Projected Training data for 2017 and 2018 includes Plateau State, and excludes Kogi State

The 17 health facilities per LGA that are supported by the Global Fund only receive SP for IPTp from PMI because SP was not included in the previous Global Fund malaria grant. For other health facilities within each LGA, PMI supports capacity building including case management training and data management support.

With the current Global Fund grant ending in December 2016, the number of unsupported health facilities will increase unless new external or domestic resources are identified. For sustainability, PMI will work with the supported states through the MOU to identify domestic funding opportunities to strengthen efforts in malaria control and reduce dependence on donor funding. By enhancing coordination with other development partners and programs, especially around logistics and data management, PMI will leverage other donor resources to reach more health facilities and people. PMI through USAID/Nigeria leadership will advocate with new state Governors to obtain state support to malaria activities in PMI-supported states.

6. Integration, collaboration, and coordination

Key international partners

Nigeria has benefited from increasing support from various partners for malaria control. Currently, the largest funding partners are the Global Fund, the USG, and United Kingdom Department for International Development (DfID). Other key partners include the United Nations Children's Fund (UNICEF) and the WHO. There is also increasing corporate sector support for malaria control including ExxonMobil, Chevron, Royal Dutch Shell, Dangote Foundation, and telecommunication companies. The Global Business Coalition through the Corporate Alliance on Malaria in Africa is galvanizing corporate efforts to support resource mobilization as well as to leverage the strength of this sector. For example, the Coca-Cola Company is working to improve logistics, while Access Bank and EcoBank group are supporting financial management.

Prior to 2014, Nigeria had three approved grants for malaria from the Global Fund, the latter two designating the NMEP as the Principal Recipient. In March 2015 the country and Global Fund signed the New Funding Model (NFM) grant totaling over $400 million for two years. The approved grant for Nigeria under the NFM is $400,253,346 to cover the period of February 2015 to December 31, 2016. The fund is managed by the NMEP ($308,577,343) and the Society for Family Health ($91,676,003) as Principal Recipients. As of the end of January 2016, $279,554,526 is already committed to support various malaria activities, including procurement of malaria commodities. The Global Fund requires the GoN to provide $45.7 million as counterpart financing for ITNs. As the current grants are expected to end by December 2016, discussions for a costed extension of the grant until December 2017 have commenced. Beyond December 2017, there is no commitment from the Global Fund to support the country's malaria program.

In terms of activities, the Global Fund grant supports scale-up of prevention and case management activities in line with the NMSP 2014-2020. The key interventions are to obtain universal coverage of ITNs through mass campaigns and continuous distribution channels; improve coverage for MIP, especially with IPTp; to increase ACT roll-out in the public and private sectors; and to increase malaria diagnosis using microscopy and RDTs in public and private health facilities. The grant also supports broader health system activities: logistics management, the HMIS, and SBCC.

The Global Fund is supporting the malaria program at the national level and in 24 states. The Global Fund and PMI collaborate in eight of the 11 PMI-supported states, and strategies are being worked out to enhance coordination and prevent duplication of efforts.

The World Bank Booster Program provided a total of about $280 million in loans between 2007 and 2009 to support seven Nigerian states and central-level malaria activities, including ITN campaigns in target states, IRS, and purchases of ACTs, RDTs, and SP for malaria control. The seven World Bank supported states are: Kano, Bauchi, Akwa Ibom, Jigawa, Rivers, Anambra, and Gombe, overlapping with PMI in Bauchi and Akwa Ibom states. The Booster Program ended in June 2013, but the project received a no-cost extension through March 2015. At present, the World Bank is exploring integrated health program implementation through performance-based financing options, private sector strengthening, and health governance support. The World Bank is also funding Saving One Million Lives (SOML), a GoN initiative designed to support at-scale delivery of evidence-based interventions and human resources for health in needed areas.

DfID supported a £89 million project (about $140 million) called Support for the National Malaria Program (SuNMaP) from 2008 to March 2016. DfID has indicated a willingness to continue funding for malaria in Nigeria but the funding levels are not yet determined beyond 2016. The program provided substantial support for the NMEP and 10 selected states, none of which overlapped with PMI's 11 states. In the DfID focus states, SuNMaP supported malaria prevention, diagnosis, and treatment, and supplied limited quantities of malaria commodities. SuNMaP developed a private sector component that examined diagnosis and treatment in the private sector, as well as a "market sector" component that addressed market interventions. DfID provided $140 million to the Global Fund to continue the subsidy for ACTs for an additional two years, through 2016.

The WHO supports a national malaria program officer in each of the six geopolitical zones of Nigeria. They assist the states in their zones with malaria program planning and management. The WHO supported the first-ever malaria program review in Nigeria in 2012. The review recommended some strategic shifts for Nigeria, such as using state-specific strategies. All PMI activities are coordinated with these efforts.

Private sector

Although PMI recognizes the potential for private sector approaches in malaria control, the opportunities to work with these organizations under PMI have been limited. Large oil firms carry out their own malaria control activities in their work areas. Some firms also include malaria control in their corporate social responsibility work. ExxonMobil funded a study on extending IPTp and other malaria interventions to community-directed distributors in Akwa Ibom State and is also supporting SBCC interventions through Malaria No More. The community IPTp study demonstrated the potential of using community-directed distributors and has helped inform PMI plans for ITN keep-up and other activities.

The Affordable Medicines Facility-malaria program of the Global Fund has transitioned into the Private Sector Co-payment Mechanism. With funding from DfID, Nigeria received approval to continue implementation of the mechanism for 2015-2016 under the Global Fund's NFM. Nigeria has 48 first-line buyers who are authorized to procure and sell the quality-assured ACTs using their distribution channels, mostly in the private sector. A total of 136 million doses of ACTs were approved to be procured in 2014. Within the approved quantities, 50% were ACTs that could be used to treat children under five years of age. For the first six months of 2015, 45 million doses were approved for the first-line buyers. The country is working through the Case

Management Sub-committee to monitor the implementation, strengthen parasite diagnosis before treatment, and improve rational drug use. There is no clear commitment for the mechanism beyond 2016.

The Private Sector Health Alliance for Millennium Development Goals includes polio and malaria as target areas for attention. This alliance is co-chaired by the state minister for health and the former chief executive officer of a Nigerian bank, and the secretariat is supported by the Dangote Foundation, the corporate social responsibility venture of one of Nigeria's most prominent businesses. The NMEP created a committee to seek private sector support, though what role the private sector will play through these actions remains unclear. There have been discussions of local production of ITNs and ACTs, but it is unlikely that they could be competitively priced.

The Corporate Alliance on Malaria in Africa, a malaria subgroup of the Global Business Coalition, is a unique coalition of companies from various industries with a common commitment to fight malaria. With co-chairs from the major industrial players in oil and gas, manufacturing, banking, and international NGOs, skills and resources are leveraged for malaria. In its second year, the annual technical forum in Nigeria aims to mobilize resources, skills, and capacity of the private sector in support of the NMSP 2014-2020.

An important malaria social marketing activity in the private sector includes the UNITAID Private Sector RDT Project, implemented in five countries. In Nigeria, UNITAID funded a one-year pilot project to create a private sector market for malaria RDTs. The objective of the project was to increase access to and demand for quality assured RDTs; improve private providers' febrile illness case management skills; and develop and implement a roadmap for public-private sector engagements that will guide policy and regulatory practices. Key interventions under the project were pricing, distribution/logistics, training and supervision, and waste management. A dissemination report indicates that there were some achievements with an improved policy environment for RDT, procurement and sale of RDT, lower median price of RDT, and trained personnel. It also recorded challenges with low demand for RDTs and potential leakages of public sector RDT into the private sector.

Within the United States Government

PMI has identified opportunities to integrate investments with other USG program activities including: within the USAID Health, Population and Nutrition team; with other USAID teams; U.S. Department of Defense (DoD); and President's Emergency Plan for AIDS Relief (PEPFAR). In mid-2013, PMI and PEPFAR agreed to collaborate on commodity storage and distribution in two states, and are considering opportunities to expand collaboration to more states. Recently, the Global Health Security Agenda (GHSA) and the USG component within GHSA were launched. The key objective of GHSA is to prevent, detect, and respond to global health threats such as infectious disease outbreaks. To achieve this, the USG is supporting efforts to strengthen the health system in the areas of capacity building, laboratories, and surveillance which will also positively impact malaria control. The PMI and GHSA teams will coordinate to ensure USG resources are maximized as health systems are strengthened with both funding streams and that efforts that benefit malaria control are coordinated under one PMI coordinated umbrella.

In 2015, PMI/Nigeria, CDC/Nigeria, the NMEP, and NFELTP/NSTOP initiated an NSTOP/Malaria Frontline project to expand the reach of U.S. Government investment in Nigeria. This project will leverage the experience in polio eradication and Ebola response to strengthen the national, state, and LGA capacity for surveillance, delivery, and monitoring of malaria interventions in Kano and Zamfara states. This project will utilize the NSTOP model to pair LGA level malaria focal persons with trained NSTOP/Malaria officers to improve surveillance, identify intervention coverage gaps, conduct supportive supervision, and provide in-service training to facility staff. In Kano, the NSTOP/Malaria Frontline project is collaborating with the GoN and DfID on implementing malaria activities. In the last 12 months, PMI supported the NSTOP/Malaria Frontline project finalized the implementation work plan and reviewed the training materials. The project has recruited key personnel including a national supervisor, a national training coordinator, and two state supervisors. The project hired 34 LGA level malaria officers. PMI assisted in the development of a malaria intervention assessment of the protocol for the baseline survey in the two states.

Support for improved malaria diagnostics has been built on the foundation established by the PEPFAR DoD-Walter Reed Program to improve human immunodeficiency virus (HIV)-related laboratory services. PMI is further expanding on this foundation to support training of trainers and the establishment of a functional malaria diagnosis quality assurance (QA) system.

PMI and PEPFAR are working to support Nigeria's integrated HMIS. This is requiring a shift from the NMEP's previous parallel system, which was created to support Global Fund reporting, and from the parallel PEPFAR system. It will take some time for the new system to become fully operational, but it is already active in several states and will eventually replace the older data reporting systems.

Steps are being taken to integrate approaches to commodity supply chain and logistics support for PEPFAR, PMI, and USAID-supported MCH and FP programs. This is particularly promising in terms of warehousing, which is a challenge in Nigeria. In four states (Ebonyi, Bauchi, Sokoto, and Zamfara), family planning and malaria funds are jointly supporting an innovative model – Direct Delivery and Information Capture (DDIC) – to improve distribution within states and collect better facility-level consumption data.

PMI is cooperating more intensively with the PEPFAR program in two states, Benue and Cross River. This cooperation includes shared warehousing and laboratory strengthening activities in the form of combined training, supervision, and QA of laboratories for malaria, HIV, and tuberculosis testing. This cooperation will expand malaria prevention and treatment programs in these two states, providing better protection of target populations.

7. PMI goal, objectives, strategic areas, and key indicators

Under the PMI Strategy for 2015-2020, the USG's goal is to work with PMI-supported countries and partners to further reduce malaria deaths and substantially decrease malaria morbidity, towards the long-term goal of elimination. Building upon the progress to date in PMI-supported countries, PMI will work with NMCPs and partners to accomplish the following objectives by 2020:

1. Reduce malaria mortality by one-third from 2015 levels in PMI-supported countries, achieving a greater than 80% reduction from PMI's original 2000 baseline levels.

2. Reduce malaria morbidity in PMI-supported countries by 40% from 2015 levels.

3. Assist at least five PMI-supported countries to meet the WHO criteria for national or sub-national pre-elimination.[2]

These objectives will be accomplished by emphasizing five core areas of strategic focus:
1. Achieving and sustaining scale of proven interventions
2. Adapting to changing epidemiology and incorporating new tools
3. Improving countries' capacity to collect and use information
4. Mitigating risk against the current malaria control gains
5. Building capacity and health systems towards full country ownership

To track progress toward achieving and sustaining scale of proven interventions (area of strategic focus #1), PMI will continue to track the key indicators recommended by the Roll Back Malaria Monitoring and Evaluation Reference Group as listed below:

- Proportion of households with at least one ITN
- Proportion of households with at least one ITN for every two people
- Proportion of children under five years old who slept under an ITN the previous night
- Proportion of pregnant women who slept under an ITN the previous night
- Proportion of households in targeted districts protected by IRS
- Proportion of children under five years old with fever in the last two weeks for whom advice or treatment was sought
- Proportion of children under five with fever in the last two weeks who had a finger or heel stick
- Proportion receiving an ACT among children under five years old with fever in the last two weeks who received any antimalarial drugs
- Proportion of women who received two or more doses of IPTp for malaria during ANC visits during their last pregnancy

---

[2] http://whqlibdoc.who.int/publications/2007/9789241596084_eng.pdf

8. Progress on coverage/impact indicators to date

Table 4: Evolution of Key Malaria Indicators in Nigeria from 2008 to 2015

Indicator	2008 NDHS	2010 NMIS	2013 NDHS	2015 NMIS
% Households with at least one ITN	8%	22%	50%	69%
% Households with at least one ITN for every two people	N/A	N/A	22%	35%
% Children under five who slept under an ITN the previous night	6%	29%	17%	44%
% Pregnant women who slept under an ITN the previous night	5%	34%	16%	49%
% Households in targeted districts protected by IRS	N/A	N/A	N/A	*1%
% Children under five years old with fever in the last two weeks for whom advice or treatment was sought	33%	49%	70%	66%
% Children under five with fever in the last two weeks who had a finger or heel stick	N/A	5%	11%	13%
% Children receiving an ACT among children under five years old with fever in the last two weeks who received any antimalarial drugs	2%	6%	18%	[+]N/A
% Women who received two or more doses of IPTp during their last pregnancy in the last two years	5%	10%	15%	37%

Notes:
*IRS data indicates 1% across the whole country, and does not disaggregate by target states. PMI discontinued IRS in 2013.
[+]Data not yet available in preliminary MIS Report

9. Other relevant evidence on progress

FMOH through the National Primary Health Care Development Agency plans to renovate and improve at least one primary health care (PHC) facility per ward in the country in next two years. If this project is completed as planned it is likely to contribute to addressing the challenges of ensuring access to the PHC system nationwide.

III. OPERATIONAL PLAN

1.   Vector monitoring and control

NMEP/PMI objectives

Vector monitoring and control falls under the preventive section of the NMSP 2014-2020. Objective One of the NMSP 2014-2020 states "At least 80% of targeted population utilizes appropriate preventive measures by 2020." The prevention strategy for the NMSP 2014-2020 includes three strategies, namely:

    i)   Integrated vector management
    ii)   Prevention of MIP; and,
    iii)   Seasonal malaria chemoprevention (SMC).

This section will discuss integrated vector management. Prevention of MIP and SMC are discussed under section 2 and the case management section.

The NMSP 2014-2020 integrated vector management strategy includes universal access to ITNs; scaling up IRS in targeted areas to interrupt malaria transmission; expanding larval source management as complementary strategies for ITNs and IRS; and vector sentinel surveillance and resistance monitoring. The use of ITNs is the primary vector control method in Nigeria as IRS is not widely implemented. The goal of the NMSP 2014-2020 is to achieve universal coverage with ITNs for the 97% of the population that is at-risk. Universal coverage is defined as one ITN for every two persons. From 2011-2013, PMI supported IRS in two LGAs in Nasarawa State to demonstrate how quality IRS can be implemented. The IRS was discontinued in 2013 and efforts refocused on entomological surveillance and insecticide resistance monitoring. PMI currently provides technical assistance, especially in environmental compliance and microplanning, to states that are implementing IRS with their own resources.

The NMSP 2014-2020 targets are:
1) At least 80% of households with at least one ITN for every two persons
2) At least 80% of children under five years of age sleep under an ITN
3) At least 80% of pregnant women sleep under an ITN
4) At least 40% of households in IRS targeted areas will be protected by 2020.
5) At least 85% of all structures in targeted LGAs will be covered using IRS during each spray cycle.
6) At least three vector surveillance sentinel sites will be established in each of the five ecological zones.

a) Entomological monitoring and insecticide resistance management

The effectiveness of IRS and ITNs is affected by mosquito behavior and insecticide susceptibility, so it is important to monitor vector population. This includes measuring indoor resting densities, biting time and location, species composition, and the insecticide resistance status. The NMSP 2014-2020 includes a strategy for vector surveillance and resistance monitoring. This activity is aimed to monitor the efficacy of insecticides used and vector susceptibility. At the request of NMEP, PMI is supporting entomological monitoring, vector mapping, and insecticide resistance monitoring of malaria vectors.

Progress since PMI was launched
PMI has supported monitoring of insecticide decay rates, indoor and outdoor mosquito collections using CDC light traps, biting activity, pyrethrum spray catch (PSC) counts, species determination, and insecticide resistance monitoring since 2011 as part of the IRS program in two LGAs of Nasarawa State. In 2013, PMI established an insectary at the Nasarawa State University in Keffi to provide susceptible mosquitoes for conducting insecticide resistance studies and to build NMEP capacity in entomological monitoring. When PMI ended its support for the IRS program, entomological surveillance was expanded to seven sites in six states of Sokoto, Nasarawa, Rivers, Enugu, Plateau, and Jigawa. The states were selected based on the five ecological zones. Nasarawa has two entomological sites that were used during the pilot IRS activities. In 2015, PMI and NMEP revised the PMI-supported entomological monitoring states to align with the PMI focus states. The number of states where entomological monitoring is taking place remained six but Rivers, Enugu, Plateau, and Jigawa sites were replaced with Akwa Ibom, Ebonyi, Oyo, and Bauchi. Therefore, the states where longitudinal entomological monitoring is taking place are: Sokoto, Nasarawa, Ebonyi, Akwa Ibom, Oyo, and Bauchi (Figure 3).

Figure 3. National and PMI-supported entomological sentinel sites, 2016

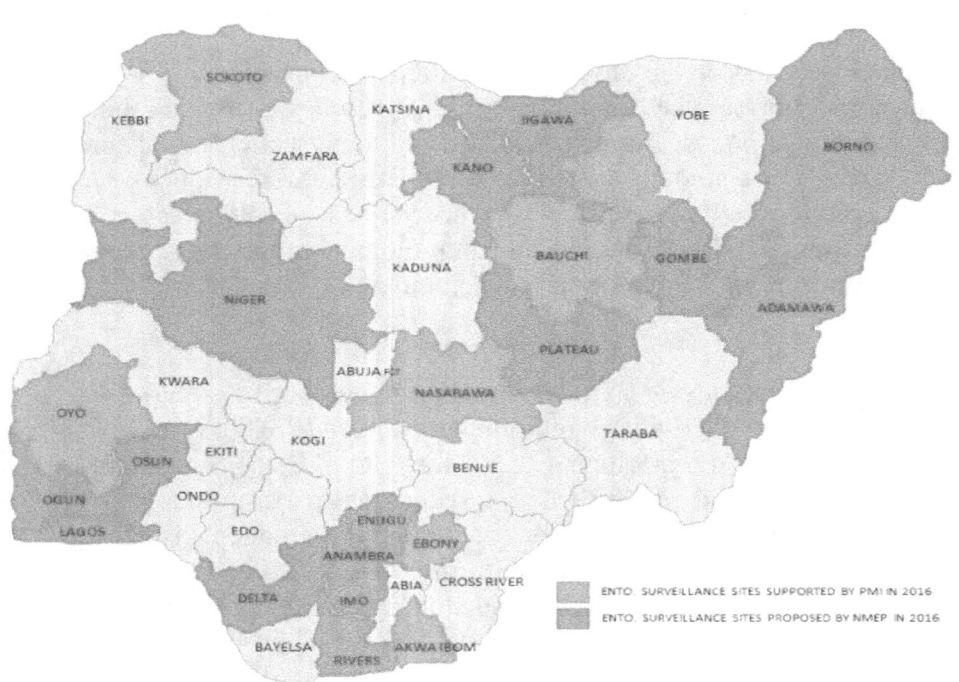

Nigeria is implementing longitudinal entomological monitoring for vector bionomics. Monitoring of vector distribution, seasonality, and other vector bionomics is done on a monthly basis in six sites, while insecticide susceptibility is done on an annual basis. Each entomological monitoring site has at least four stations for insecticide susceptibility testing. A surveillance station refers to the points for collection of larvae for susceptibility testing. These sites have been conducting biennial susceptibility monitoring of four classes of WHO Pesticide Evaluation Scheme (WHOPES)-recommended ITN and IRS insecticides. The insecticides tested are organochlorines, organophosphates, pyrethroids, and carbamates. The IRS demonstration activity and the entomological monitoring guided the design of the additional entomological sites in the country. CDC bottle intensity bioassays, oxidase enzyme testing for resistance mechanisms, and vector bionomics monitoring began in late 2014. PMI has continued and intensified entomological surveillance in six states (Figure 3).

Progress during the past 12-18 months
PMI-supported mosquito surveillance included indoor resting densities (IRDs) with PSC and CDC light/human-baited traps to determine mosquito biting time and to conduct speciation. From November 2014 to December 2015, a significantly higher numbers of *An. gambiae s.l.* were collected indoors than outdoors across the six sentinel sites. The primary vector reported was *An. gambiae* s.l., but with *An. funestus* reported in high numbers from two sentinel sites (Enugu and Plateau). The highest indoor biting peak was reported from the Sokoto site. ELISA

analysis for sporozoite infection indicated that infection rate was highest (7.8%) in Sokoto, followed by Enugu (6.6%), and Lagos (5.5%). In the Nasarawa sentinel site only 1.8% of the samples were positive for *Plasmodium* infection. On insecticide resistance, both WHO tube tests and CDC bottle bioassay methods were used to determine the susceptibility level of the vector population across the different ecological zones. The local mosquitoes (*An. gambiae* s.l) were found to show resistance to DDT (organochlorine) across the six sentinel sites. *An. gambiae* s.l. showed resistance to the pyrethroids (lambdacyhalothrin, deltamethrin, and permethrin) across all sites, although susceptibility to alphacypermethrin was observed in Rivers. In the carbamate class, susceptibility to bendiocarb was observed across all sentinel sites except Sokoto State while propoxur and pirimiphos methyl (organophosphate) was susceptible in Lagos but suspected resistance was recorded in Plateau and Enugu sentinel sites. This study shows that although pyrethroid resistance is widespread, the intensity of the resistance in Nigeria is not high. The low mortality for the tests on pirimiphos methyl across the different sites could be due to problems with the stability of insecticides used for the tests.

Resistance intensity assays showed variations in intensity across the six sentinel sites. There was high intensity resistance to deltamethrin (survival at 5X and 10X dosage in three sentinel sites of Lagos, Plateau, and Rivers), while susceptibility at 2X was observed in Enugu, Nasarawa, and Sokoto.

Synergist assays were performed using PBO, an inhibitor of monoxygenase, in two sites (Nasarawa and Lagos) and findings showed that mosquitoes were susceptible in Nasarawa N/Eggon with mortality of 98.8% (n = 100); in Lagos susceptibility to deltamethrin was partially restored in the deltamethrin after exposure to PBO. This indicates that in Lagos monoooxygenases might not be the only resistant mechanism involved.

The NMEP and partners have identified 18 sentinel sites for entomological monitoring, out of which 6 are functional; all are funded by PMI. Currently NMEP is soliciting support from other donors to support the remaining 12 sentinel sites.

PMI supported training of entomologists and entomological technicians from the NMEP and the six PMI funded sentinel sites. These trainees are now conducting surveillance activities in the various sentinel sites. The capacity and data generated from PMI supported sentinel sites has been used to develop vector distribution and insecticide resistance profile. The data on insecticide resistance has strengthened the fact that ITNs are still effective and also discouraged the use of DDT in the states that are implementing IRS.

PMI supported capacity building of GoN personnel, particularly at the NMEP, to provide consistent entomological monitoring activities as part of their annual malaria intervention plan. Staff members who were trained in insecticide resistance testing in 2014 received follow-up training on the CDC bottle bioassay in August 2015 with the support of PMI.

Table 5: *Anopheles gambiae s.l.* **mortality rates (%) using the WHO Tube Bioassay Method to eight insecticides from six locations in Nigeria, 2015.**

Insecticide	Class*	Plateau	Sokoto	Rivers	Enugu	Nasarawa Doma	Nasarawa Eggon	Lagos
Permethrin	P	97	30	58	19	10	50	12
Deltamethrin	P	74	83	40	84	59	85	7
α-cypermethrin	P	84	68	98	68	85	89	96
Lambdacyhalothrin	P	88	12	48	13	23	35	12
DDT	OC	43	70	37	6	7	8	1
Bendiocarb	C	100	73	100	100	100	100	100
Propoxur	C	95	NA	78	95	NA	NA	98
Pirimiphos-methyl	OP	74	63	59	52	100	95	100

*P= Pyrethroid, C= Carbamate, OC= Organochlorine, OP = Organophosphate
Source: AIRS Nigeria Final Entomology Report. November 2014 – December 2015

Plans and justification

With FY 2017 funds, PMI will continue to support the NMEP to conduct mosquito surveillance and insecticide resistance training. Currently, NMEP and its partners have identified 21 entomological monitoring sites, although entomology capacity is still concentrated in Nasarawa and Lagos. Capacity needs to be broadened throughout the country. The NMEP has been seeking other donor support to expand entomological monitoring.

As part of PMI's strategic review process, four PMI-supported entomological monitoring sites were re-located to correspond with PMI-supported states. The Sokoto and Nasarawa sites have continued. While the scope of PMI operations may change, the number of states supported for entomological monitoring is expected to remain at six. Each site will have four surveillance "stations" to provide a consistent assessment of the vector population. Stations will include both pyrethrum spray catches and CDC light traps.

PMI support to the NMEP entomological monitoring activities will aim specifically to characterize insecticide susceptibility, spatial and temporal composition and distribution of anopheline species, assist with vector mapping using Geographic Information Systems, support the expansion of the insectary, and continue to provide technical assistance to NMEP. Laboratory tests for mosquito infection rates will be conducted with polymerase chain reaction (PCR) at the National Institute of Medical Research, Lagos. This will also provide valuable information to determine if PMI control initiatives are affecting vector infection rates.

Proposed activities with FY 2017 funding ($1,059,000):

1. Provide support for vector surveillance and susceptibility monitoring across four ecological zones in Nigeria: Supervision, entomological monitoring, vehicle rentals, and equipment to survey malaria vectors in six sites around the country once a year. *($680,000)*

2. Strengthen capacity for entomological expertise at federal and state levels. Strengthen capacity for entomological competence at national and state levels with training and equipment support (WHO cone wall bioassays, light trap collections, pyrethrum spray collections, surveillance equipment training, larval surveillance, and insecticide susceptibility training). Maintain an insectary in Nasarawa State. *($350,000)*

3. CDC technical assistance to NMEP on entomology activities. Two trips to provide insecticide resistance training for Nigerian IRS staff, resistance test kits, and insecticide for Nigerian vector control officers attending training. Training and technical assistance to primary investigators involved in the sentinel surveillance project with implementing partners. *($29,000)*

b. Insecticide-treated nets

The NMEP ITN strategy identifies mass campaigns and four continuous distribution channels, namely:

1) Mass free distributions of nets repeated every three years;
2) Continuous distribution through:
   a. Routine health services: ANC and expanded program on immunization (EPI) clinics;
   b. School-based distributions;
   c. Community-based distribution; and,
   d. Social marketing through the commercial sector.

The ITN mass campaigns are conducted every three years in all the 36 states plus the Federal Capital Territory. Continuous ITN distribution through ANC and EPI clinics has been occurring and is supported by PMI in 11 states. The ITN strategies are complemented with the monitoring of use and durability of ITNs, and social and behavior change communication (SBCC) that is discussed under section 5 of the malaria operational plan.

As part of the strategic review process in 2014, PMI joined the NMEP and partners to review the available evidence to determine the most effective mix of distribution channels to reach the highest number of people. ANC/EPI attendance varies by zone, with significantly lower attendance in northern states. Despite these low ANC/EPI attendance rates, the NMEP is committed to including ITNs as part of a comprehensive ANC package of services in order to strengthen the overall service delivery platform that health facilities provide. The NMEP and partners support adding school and community distribution channels to ANC/EPI efforts. Ideally, scaling up continuous distribution channels—ANC, EPI, and either schools or communities—will reduce reliance on mass campaigns for achieving and maintaining high coverage.

PMI's goal is to support the NMEP in achieving and maintaining its targets for ITN coverage and use, especially in PMI-supported states. PMI supports mass free ITN campaigns, strengthening ANC and EPI channels for routine distribution, and adding school or community-based distribution where feasible and cost-effective.

Mass ITN campaigns will be required in Nigeria in order to achieve and maintain universal coverage for the foreseeable future. The ANC/EPI channels are not sufficient, and adding school and community channels will take time. The PMI supported states can be grouped into three categories: 1. Low ANC/EPI and low school attendance; 2. Moderate ANC/EPI and moderate school attendance; 3. High ANC/EPI and high school attendance.

PMI/Nigeria's ITN approach is based on a state's category:

- Group 1: These states will be heavily dependent on mass campaigns. PMI will support ANC/EPI distribution in high volume facilities (low ANC/EPI attendance is not uniform throughout the state), and PMI will support gradually adding community distribution channels.
- Group 2: These states will require mass campaigns. PMI will support ANC/EPI distributions in all health facilities. PMI will support gradually adding community distribution channels or schools.
- Group 3: These states will require at least one more full universal coverage mass campaign. Subsequent mass campaigns might be transitioned to top-up campaigns depending on the success of the continuous channels. PMI will support ANC/EPI distributions in all health facilities. PMI will support gradually adding school distributions in all LGAs.

Table 6: Nigeria ITN Mass and Continuous Distribution Strategy in PMI-supported States

Group	State	Projected population 2018	ANC Attendance (2013 NDHS)	Measles Coverage (2013 NDHS)	**Net Primary School Attendance Ratio	ITN distribution channels			
						Mass campaign (year)	ANC+	EPI+	School or community
1	Kebbi	4,735,848	24%	34%	31%	2014	X	X	Community
	Sokoto	5,297,612	17%	33%	31%	2017	X	X	Community
	Zamfara	4,784,989	22%	35%	35%	2015	X	X	Community
2	Bauchi	6,941,952	56%	47%	41%	2014	X	X	Community
	Benue	6,092,998	57%	77%	71%	2015	X	X	Community
	Nasarawa	2,680,852	63%	71%	73%	2014	X	X	Community
	*Plateau	4,539,891	63%	47%	66%	2015	X	X	TBD
3	Akwa Ibom	5,801,268	73%	75%	83%	2014	X	X	School
	Cross River	4,072,158	73%	74%	78%	2015	X	X	School
	Ebonyi	3,039,338	85%	86%	83%	2015	X	X	School
	Oyo	8,287,615	87%	64%	74%	2016	X	X	School
	TOTAL	**56,274,521**							

+PMI targets health facilities with high outpatient load and ANC attendance.
* PMI support for Kogi state will end with FY 2015 funds
*PMI will commence support to Plateau State starting with FY2016 funds. Plateau State efforts will initially focus on ANC/EPI channels with a community continuous channel unlikely before 2020
** National Education Data Survey Percentage of official primary school age population that attend primary school. Data obtained from 2015 NEDS.

Progress since PMI was launched
PMI has supported routine ITN distribution through ANC and EPI clinics from the start. However, routine ITN distribution has been limited to health facilities that are receiving PMI or Global Fund support.

Nigeria started piloting the school distribution channel in 2012 and the community-based distribution channels in 2013. The community channel is also being used to provide ITNs for internally displaced persons (IDPs) from the conflicts in the northeastern states. Based on lessons learned, Nigeria is refining these two channels to expand more broadly. States have an option of distributing ITNs through schools or community to supplement the routine distribution through

ANC and EPI clinics. Distribution channels are adapted at state level to ensure a manageable level of specification is achieved.

Since 2011, PMI has procured a total of 32 million ITNs for mass campaigns and continuous distribution, and distributed approximately 56 million ITNs; including over 24 million ITNs procured by other partners and distributed using PMI funds. From December 2013 to May 2015, the NMEP and its partners distributed 58 million ITNs through mass campaigns in 17 states, including over 15 million ITNs in the eight PMI-supported states of Sokoto, Bauchi, Nasarawa, Kebbi, Cross River, Ebonyi, Zamfara, and Benue.

As detailed in the "Progress on Coverage/Impact Indicators" section, data from NMIS and NDHS show ownership of at least one ITN in a household increased substantially from 8% the in 2010 NMIS to 69% in 2015 NMIS (Figure 4).

Figure 4: Trends in ITN Ownership by Residence (Percent of households with at least one ITN)

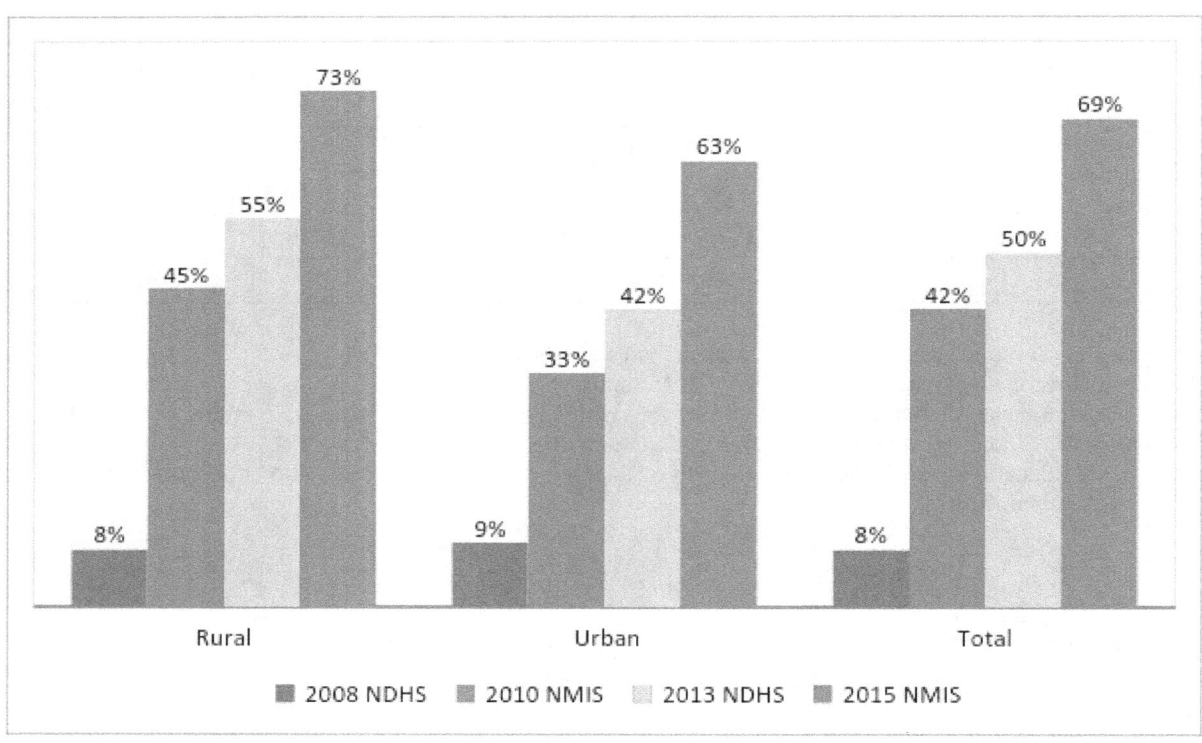

The average number of ITNs per household doubled from 0.8 in 2010 NMIS to 1.6 in 2015 NMIS. Eight of the eleven PMI-supported states had a higher ownership of at least one ITN per household than the national average. The three states that had a lower ITN ownership than the national average are Oyo, Kogi, and Benue, which will conduct mass ITN campaigns in 2016 (Figure 5).

Figure 5: Percentage of households with at least one ITN, in the 11 PMI Focus States (2015 NMIS)

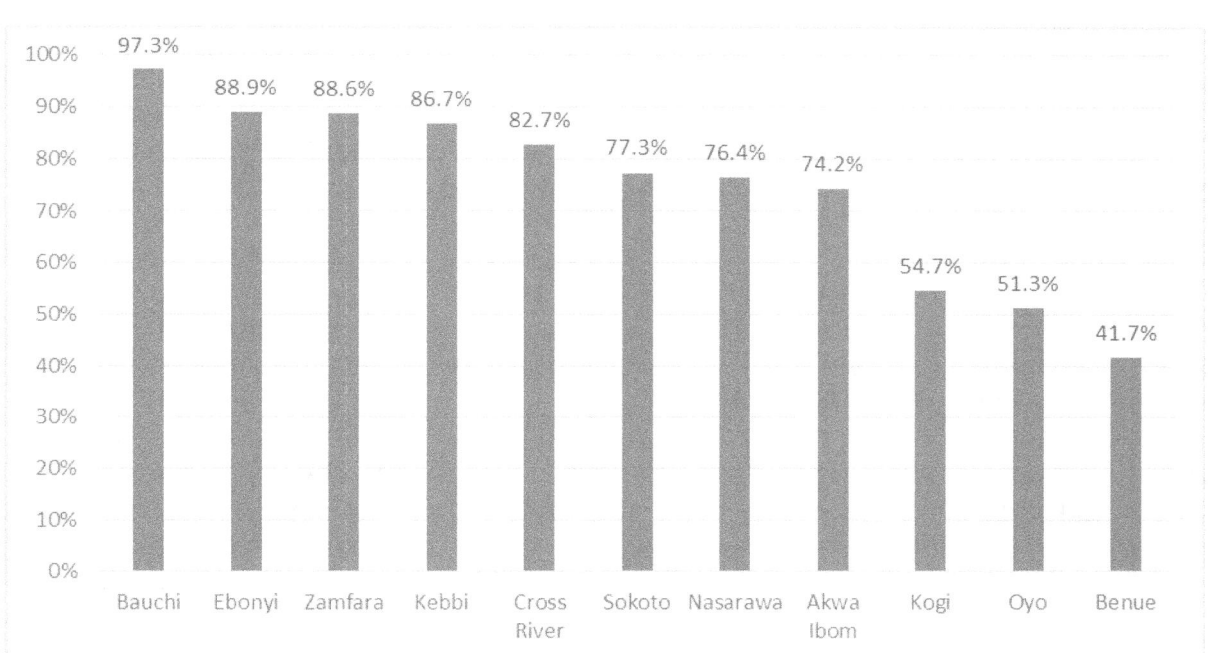

Mean national percentage of households with at least one ITN = 68.8%

The percentage households with at least one ITN for every two people increased from 22% in 2013 NDHS to 35% in 2015 NMIS. The percentage of the total population that slept under an ITN increased from 23% in 2010 to 37% in 2015 NMIS. The percentage of population that slept under an ITN in households owning at least in one ITN did not change between 2010 (49%) and 2015 (50%). For children under five years of age and pregnant women, net use in households with ITNs was 59% and 65% in 2010 NMIS, respectively; in 2015 NMIS, it decreased slightly to 57% for children under five years of age and 62% in pregnant women. PMI Nigeria with the NMEP and partners will further analyze the NMIS 2015 results and investigate why improved access to ITNs did not result in increased ITN use.

There is evidence to show that Nigeria has addressed inequities in ITN ownership and use. The 2010 NMIS and 2015 NMIS data consistently show higher net ownership and use in the poorer northern Nigeria and the rural populations, compared to the southern Nigeria and the urban populations. The 2015 NMIS data also show higher ITN ownership among the low wealth quintiles compared to high wealth quantile (86% vs. 58%).

39

PMI initiated a community-based distribution system through Community Drug Distributors in in 2013, in 52 health facilities of Nasarawa State. A household survey conducted in April 2014[3] found that household occupants who were aware of the community-based distribution program were significantly more likely to have adequate ITN access than those unaware of the service. However, program effectiveness was low, with only 18% of households aware of the channel. Challenges encountered included stockouts of nets or net coupons and lack of understanding of the new scheme. Although the pilot results were less than expected, the NMEP and PMI opted to use the results as a framework for expanding community-based channels in select states.

To complement existing approaches, particularly in areas where ANC uptake is low, PMI supported pilots of both community- and school-based ITN distribution channels. In determining distribution methods, the NMEP, with PMI support, used community-based distribution in states with lower school attendance and high dropout rates, and school-based distribution in states with high school attendance and low dropout rates.

In 2012, PMI supported a school-based ITN distribution pilot in two LGAs of Cross River State. Collaborating closely with LGA education departments, PMI facilitated distribution through March 2014 of over 55,000 ITNs among four grade levels in 192 schools, reaching 95% of eligible children. An end-line evaluation survey in March 2014 showed that population access in households increased from 34% to 55% in the two LGAs with school-based distribution, versus decreasing from 38% to 26% in a control LGA with ANC distribution alone. In addition, ownership of at least one ITN reached between 76% and 77% in the two intervention LGAs, a 25% increase since 2012. This contrasts with a decrease in ownership from 50% to 43% in the control LGA. In 2014 and 2015, PMI continued supporting school-based distribution in Cross River State, and expanded to Oyo State. Through this effort, 126,654 nets have been distributed in schools in these two states.

Alongside the piloting of school and community-based distribution channels, PMI supported an ITN durability monitoring study to assess the physical integrity and attrition of ITNs in Nigeria. The PMI-funded net durability study in three states demonstrated that variance in the survival of a 100-denier polyester ITN among sites was driven by three extrinsic variables: living conditions, attitudes, and household behavior. The median net survival among states ranged from 3.0 to 4.7 years. Net-hole damage was commonly caused by pulling it (mechanical damage), rodent bites, and open flame. The results informed future plans and protocols for routine ITN durability monitoring.[4]

---

[3] Albert Kilian and Emmanuel Obi: Community-Based, Continuous Distribution of LLIN in Nasarawa State, Nigeria. Report prepared for VectorWorks by Tropical Health LLP and Johns Hopkins Center for Communication Programs, August 6, 2015.

[4] Albert Kilian, Hannah Koenker, Emmanuel Obi, Richmond Selby, Megan Fotheringham, and Matthew Lynch: Field durability of the same type of long-lasting insecticidal net varies between regions in Nigeria due to differences in household behaviour and living conditions. *Malaria Journal* (2015) 14:123

A study on net repair, maintenance, and care practices and their effect on ITN longevity was also carried out in Nasarawa State between March 2012 and April 2014.[6] The study found that while the comprehensive communication intervention improved attitudes and behaviors about the care and repair of nets, these efforts had little effect on overall net lifespan. While repair to damaged nets can be induced by changing attitudes towards repair, more effort should focus on preventive behavior, such as folding or tying up the net after use, and avoiding storage of food in the same room. A comprehensive SBCC intervention to promote these behaviors was incorporated into existing PMI malaria communication interventions.

Progress during the last 12-18 months
With FY 2015 funds, PMI procured 9,732,500 ITNs, out of which 7,732,500 were designated for mass campaigns and 2 million for continuous distribution. The three states that conducted ITN mass campaigns were Cross River, Ebonyi, and Zamfara, with over 95% of registered households receiving a net. Due to the ongoing crisis in northeastern Nigeria and the migration of IDPs, PMI donated over 558,570 ITNs for distribution to IDPs living in camps in 2015.

In addition, all 11 PMI-supported states of Bauchi, Sokoto, Zamfara, Kebbi, Nasarawa, Kogi, Oyo, Benue, Ebonyi, Cross River, and Akwa Ibom are distributing ITNs through ANC at first ANC visit and through EPI clinics with measles vaccination. As stated earlier, PMI is targeting health facilities with high outpatient load and ANC attendance for support. With FY 2015 funds, PMI procured 2 million ITNs for routine distribution through ANC and EPI clinics, and community or school distribution. In 2014 and 2015, PMI supported the five states of Benue, Kogi, Ebonyi, Nasarawa, and Zamfara to conduct community-based distribution of ITNs, and Oyo and Cross River states to distribute ITNs through schools. In total, with PMI support, the above states distributed 455,442 ITNs through the community channel, and 126,654 through schools. However, the community and school distribution channels are still on a limited scale; they will be expanded with FY 2016 funds.

In 2015, routine data from seven PMI-supported states indicated that about 65% of women received an ITN during their first ANC visits at a public facility. Field visits confirm that ITN distribution through this channel functions well in some of the states especially where ANC attendance is high. The quality of record-keeping is variable, complicated by the register design. Clinic registers include a column for ANC-based distribution but not for EPI.

With FY 2015 funding, PMI started ITN durability monitoring in Zamfara, Oyo, and Ebonyi states to assess ITNs for attrition, physical integrity, and insecticidal effectiveness over a 36-month period. Durability monitoring is being conducted in one site per state, and each site is aligned with the entomological monitoring sites in each state. Baseline data collection and recruitment of a cohort of nets was conducted in Ebonyi and Zamfara in February to March 2016. In total, 374 and 360 campaign nets were recruited in Ebonyi and Zamfara, respectively. The baseline for Oyo is awaiting the ITN mass campaign scheduled for the end June 2016.

Commodity gap analysis

With FY 2017 funds, PMI will support the distribution of ITNs through: a) mass campaigns and b) continuous distribution through ANC and EPI clinics, schools, and community structures. The timing of mass ITN campaigns is based on projected replacement needs every three years. The table below presents the gap analysis for the PMI-supported states by distribution channel.

Table 7. ITN Gap Analysis (2016-2018)

Calendar Year	2016	2017	2018
Total country population	192,935,362	199,220,487	205,723,765
Total Targeted Population (PMI-supported)	52,885,275	54,553,493	56,274,521
Continuous Distribution Needs			
ANC (60%)	2,367,399	2,443,155	2,521,336
EPI (15%)	591,850	610,789	630,334
Others (Community/School based) (25%)	986,416	1,017,981	1,050,557
Estimated Total Need for Continuous	3,945,665	4,071,926	4,202,227
Mass Distribution Needs			
Mass distribution campaign	9,970,622	7,900,000	9,601,729
Estimated Total Need for Campaigns	9,970,622	7,900,000	9,601,729
Emergency distribution need for Internally displaced persons			
ITN need for internally displaced persons	0	300,000	400,000
Total Calculated Need: Continuous and Campaign	13,916,286	12,271,926	14,203,956
Partner Contributions			
ITNs carried over from previous year	2,875,198	916,122	364,756
ITNs from Government	0	0	0
ITNs from Global Fund Round	2,020,560	2,020,560	2,020,560
ITNs from Other Donors	0	0	0
ITNs planned with PMI funding	9,936,650	9,700,000	8,255,722
Total ITNs Available	14,832,408	12,636,682	10,641,038
Total ITN Surplus (Gap)	916,122	364,756	(3,562,918)

Assumptions:

- The population derived using from 2016 census using growth rate of 3.2%. NetCalc used to estimate quantity of routine nets using population estimates and the following assumptions: estimated number of women likely to become pregnant is 5% of the population.

- The average public sector ANC attendance in the 11 PMI focus states is 60%, and estimated average EPI measles coverage is 85%. An estimated 3% of households will be reached by other routine distribution channels (community and school distribution channels).

- The resulting total number for continuous distribution is allocated between ANC, EPI and others using 60% for ANC, 15% for EPI, and 25% for other methods (e.g. community based distribution).

- Estimates for ITN mass campaigns are obtained by dividing the population in PMI states due for campaigns in 2016, 2017, and 2018 by 1.8 (to achieve 1 net per 2 people ratio). Benue, Oyo, and Kogi ITN mass campaigns will take place May-August 2016; Sokoto, Kebbi, and Nasarawa in 2017; and Bauchi, Akwa Ibom, and Plateau State in 2018.

- Global Fund ITN procurements for the PMI-supported states are flat-lined. The current malaria grant is ending December 2016. NMEP program is currently negotiating with the Global Fund for an extension.

- The security situation has deteriorated resulting in more IDPs requiring increased PMI support.

Plans and justification

PMI will continue to support the national malaria strategy in conducting both ITN mass campaigns and expanding existing and appropriate new channels for continuous distribution. Routine distribution through ANC and EPI clinics will be complemented by expansion of school and community-based distribution channels. PMI will work with the NMEP and state-level programs to determine the most effective strategy for scaling up continuous distribution channels. Bauchi and Akwa Ibom States held ITN mass campaigns in 2014, thus both are due for mass campaigns in 2018 with FY 2017 funds. Plateau State had a mass campaign in March 2015 and therefore will also be due for a mass campaign in 2018. However, FY 2017 funds can only cover the two mass campaigns in Bauchi and Akwa Ibom states, and 1,176,155 ITNs for routine distribution, leaving an ITN gap of 3,562,918 (Plateau 2,522,162, continuous distribution 1,040756). PMI/Nigeria is advocating to the NMEP and the Global Fund to support Plateau State's ITN mass campaign for 2018. If Global Fund procures the ITNs, PMI will support the distribution and other operational costs for the mass campaign.

The civil unrest in Nigeria has greatly affected and displaced a significant population in Northern Nigeria. Some PMI-supported states like Benue also experience internal conflicts that result in displacing populations from their residences. The IDPs are at risk of increased malaria transmission. The USG humanitarian response strategy includes distribution of ITNs to the displaced populations.

Multi-channel SBCC efforts will be significantly increased to address the demographic and regional variations in ITN use. Using the findings of the 2015 NMIS and the results from the 2014 study on net care and repair, PMI will help develop, effectively target (geographically and by population group), and intensify national and local communications strategies to improve net preventive care and year-round net use in households.

43

To verify the quality and effectiveness of ITN products distributed, PMI will continue to support the monitoring of ITN physical integrity, attrition/survivorship, and insecticide content and effectiveness. The durability monitoring will take place in the three states of Zamfara, Oyo, and Ebonyi. The states were selected in consultation with NMEP and IVM partners. The durability monitoring is linked to mass distribution campaigns. The results will inform both future net replacement strategies and communication approaches to promote proper care of nets.

The substantial gaps both for continuous distribution and mass campaigns are a major concern for PMI and its partners. PMI will work with the NMEP and other partners to advocate for additional funding, particularly from federal and state resources. The NMEP will need to prioritize identifying matching funds to the Global Fund contribution to ITN campaigns.

Proposed activities with FY 2017 funding ($31,467,000):

1. Procure approximately 8,255,722 ITNs with FY 2017 funds. A total of 7,079,567 ITNs will be used to support ITN mass campaigns in Bauchi (3,856,640), Akwa Ibom (3,222,927), and the balance of 1,176,155 ITNs will be used for continuous distribution needs in all 11 PMI-supported states of Bauchi, Sokoto, Zamfara, Kebbi, Nasarawa, Oyo, Benue, Ebonyi, Cross River, Akwa Ibom and Plateau and to the internally displaced persons. Cost includes transport from manufacturer to state warehouses. *($23,776,480)*

2. Distribution of ITNs through continuous channels: Distribute 1,176,155 ITNs from state warehouses to service delivery points in the 11 PMI-supported states of Bauchi, Sokoto, Zamfara, Kebbi, Nasarawa, Oyo, Benue, Ebonyi, Cross River, Akwa Ibom and Plateau. *($1,000,000)*

3. ITN mass campaigns: Implement ITN mass campaigns in Bauchi and Akwa Ibom States (7,079,567 ITNs). This includes the distribution of ITNs from state warehouses to various distribution points, microplanning, training, household registration, development and procuring campaign materials, distribution of nets to beneficiaries through a network of volunteers, data collection and analysis, and report writing. This does not include SBCC costs for mass campaigns that are budgeted under the SBCC section. *($6,490,520)*

4. Support for SBCC for malaria prevention: PMI will support SBCC activities, including interpersonal communication (IPC), mass media, and social mobilization to promote ITN ownership and use, as well as other key aspects of malaria control and prevention. (*Costs included in cross-cutting activities described in the SBCC section.*)

5. ITN Durability Monitoring: PMI will conduct ITN durability monitoring at three sites in three states to monitor the integrity, attrition, and survivorship of ITNs. This activity is included in SM&E table. *($200,000)*

c. Indoor Residual Spraying

Progress since PMI was launched

In 2011, PMI started support for a two-year IRS pilot activity in two local government areas of Nasarawa State. This IRS pilot program was designed as a demonstration spray program for MoH and local officials to see high-quality IRS implementation which was underpinned by reliable entomological surveillance and capacity building. During the two years of actual spraying, about 150,000 households were sprayed, protecting over 346,000 people each year in the two LGAs. The IRS demonstration activity and the entomological monitoring guided the design of the additional entomological sites in the country.

During the same period, the NMEP, with funding from the World Bank Booster Program, conducted IRS in 6 of the 7 Booster Program states (no overlap with PMI focus states), in a total of 14 LGAs. This IRS program also had an entomological monitoring component which was implemented in collaboration with research institutions in the country. The World Bank Booster program ended in March 2014 and most states did not have domestic resources to continue IRS activities. The exception was Lagos, which has consistently conducted IRS since 2009 in two LGAs, although the last spray round in 2015 was delayed due to changes in political leadership in the state.

Among the corporate organizations, Chevron and Shell have conducted IRS in their drilling communities protecting both staff residential quarters and community catchment areas as part of their corporate social responsibility and desire to protect the health of their employees and their families. The Ministry of Defense has also conducted IRS in the military residential communities.

PMI is not actively conducting IRS and there is no IRS activity in any of the PMI-supported states. To support the entomological monitoring for IRS activities, in 2013, PMI set up an insectary at the Nasarawa State University in Keffi. The insectary provides susceptible mosquitoes for measuring IRS insecticide decay rates and can now support current state-managed IRS activities.

Table 8: PMI-supported IRS activities 2011 - 2013

Calendar Year	Number of Districts* Sprayed	Insecticide Used	Number of Structures Sprayed	Coverage Rate	Population Protected
2011	2 LGA	Pyrethroid	58,704	99.1%	346,115
2012	2 LGA	Pyrethroid	62,526	100%	346,544

Progress during the past 12-18 months
Although some state governments and the private companies have shown interest in implementing IRS, there has not been measurable progress in IRS program in the recent years. The World Bank Booster Project funded IRS program closed in 2013 and the seven World Bank-supported states (Kano, Bauchi, Akwa Ibom, Jigawa, Rivers, Anambra, and Gombe) have not been able to implement IRS without external support.

PMI provides support for building the capacity of the GoN personnel, particularly at the NMEP, to provide consistent entomological monitoring activities as part of their annual malaria intervention. Staff members who were trained in insecticide resistance testing in 2014 received follow-up training on the CDC bottle bioassay in August 2015 using PMI funds.

Plans and justification
With the release of the 2015 NMIS preliminary results, IRS scale up may become a priority for the NMEP and some states. The report indicates that states in the North West have high prevalence despite high ITN ownership and use, and NMEP may recommend IRS to these states. Other states (not PMI-supported) have also communicated interest in conducting IRS to the NMEP and some have requested technical support in planning and implementation.

Proposed activities with FY 2017 funding: ($50,000)
Technical assistance to NMEP and PMI focus on IRS activities: A number of states including Lagos are currently doing some IRS and PMI funding will be used to provide technical assistance and capacity strengthening to the NMEP to support these states to conduct high quality IRS, and to develop an insecticide resistance management plan. *($50,000)*

2. Malaria in pregnancy

NMEP/PMI objectives

Nigeria implements all three interventions recommended by WHO for the prevention and treatment of MIP:

1. Use of long-lasting insecticidal nets

2. IPTp with SP
3. Prompt diagnosis and effective treatment of malaria illness.

High transmission rates and variable ANC attendance and ITN use in pregnancy have added to the high burden of malaria during pregnancy. The total population has been projected to be over 205 million in 2018, with an estimated 10.3 million pregnancies annually. The NMSP 2014-2020 emphasizes that MIP interventions are a component of the focused ante-natal care (FANC) services delivered by Reproductive/Maternal/Child Health Units within the Federal Ministry of Health. However, coordination of MIP activities is the responsibility of the NMEP through the MIP Technical Working Group (TWG) in collaboration with the Family Health Department, both located within the FMoH.

The NMSP 2014-2020 targets for MIP are:

1) At least 80% of pregnant women will sleep inside ITNs.
2) All (100%) of eligible pregnant women attending ANC receive at least three doses of SP-IPTp by 2020 through directly observed therapy (DOT).
3) Eighty percent of pregnant women with fever and malaria receive appropriate and timely treatment according to the national treatment guidelines by 2017, and 100% by 2020.

Intermittent preventive treatment for pregnant women

In 2014, Nigeria adopted the updated WHO IPTp policy of providing IPTp with SP, starting as early as possible in the second trimester, for all pregnant women at each scheduled antenatal care visit until the time of delivery, provided that the doses are given at least one month apart. The IPTp SP is to be administered as DOT during ANC visits. The NMEP and partners have revised the training and SBCC materials

Table 9: Status of implementation of IPTp policy

WHO Policy updated to reflect 2012 guidance	Status of training on updated IPTp policy	Number of HCW trained on new policy in the last year	Are the revised guidelines available at the facility level?	ANC register updated to capture 3 doses of IPTp-SP	HMIS/ DHIS2 updated to capture 3 doses of IPTp-SP
2014	Activity is a continuous process.	3,098 (cumulatively, 60% of ANC healthcare workers in focus states)	Guidelines are available in PMI supported health facilities	In process. Estimated Completion Date: June 2017	In process. Estimated Completion Date: June 2017

Iron / Folate
The national guidelines and strategies for malaria prevention and control during pregnancy states that SP shall be administered as part of the ANC package with other components including anti-helminthics in the second or third trimester, nutrition counselling, and daily hematinic supplements (iron and low dose folic acid). Because high dose folic acid is still procured and provided at ANC in Nigeria, the guideline recommends that since SP is an anti-folate, high dose folic acid should be withheld for one week after SP administration.

ITNs
Under the NMSP 2014-2020, one of the distribution channels for improving and sustaining access to ITNs is to provide an ITN to every pregnant woman during the first ANC visit. Support from PMI is discussed in the ITN section.

Management of acute malaria
According to Nigeria's National Guidelines for Diagnosis and Treatment of Malaria (2011), the recommendation for treating uncomplicated MIP is quinine + clindamycin for the first trimester and an ACT for the second and third trimesters. For severe malaria, the guidelines recommend using injectable artesunate (IAS) (or intravenous quinine if IAS is not available). Quinine is on the essential medicines list and is readily available in country.

Progress since PMI was launched

PMI has supported a MIP strategy that includes IPTp, ITNs through ANC, and prompt case management of malaria during pregnancy. Efforts have focused on increasing IPTp coverage through provision of free SP to pregnant women in ANC clinics, scaling up ITN distribution to pregnant women during the first ANC visit, and testing and promptly treating pregnant women with confirmed malaria.

To improve IPTp coverage and access to SP, PMI has procured 13 million treatments of SP since FY 2012, of which 5 million treatment doses have been distributed. Additionally, PMI has supported the training of over 3,000 health workers in MIP, and distributed over 100,000 ITNs through the ANC clinics as part of the FANC package. To improve coverage and performance of MIP interventions in Nigeria, PMI supports capacity building and supervision of service providers to improve delivery of FANC services in the 11 PMI-supported states. The training includes IPC to improve behavior and attitudes of service providers towards IPTp. Community-level SBCC activities are being implemented across states to improve ANC attendance by pregnant women.

Investments in MIP by PMI and other partners over the years are yielding results. Nigeria has increased ITN ownership at household level, with a corresponding increase in use by pregnant women. According to the 2015 NMIS, more households own at least one ITN – 69% (compared to 42% in 2010), and 49% of pregnant women age 15-49 in all households slept inside an ITN the night before the survey; in 2010, only 28% of pregnant women age 15-49 slept inside a treated net.

The 2013 NDHS showed that 61% of pregnant women attended ANC with a skilled health worker and 51% of pregnant women had four or more ANC visits. However, the ANC attendance was relatively low in states located in northern Nigeria. The 2015 NMIS showed that 46% of pregnant women received any IPTp compared to 15% in 2010 (NMIS), 37% received two or more doses of IPTp compared to 13% in 2010, and 19% received three or more doses of SP as compared to 6% in 2013 (NDHS).

The 2015 NMIS also showed women in urban areas were more likely to have received at least one dose of IPTp (63%) than women in the rural areas (38%). A mother's education, wealth quintile, and urban or rural residence have been identified as factors affecting IPTp uptake. Pregnant women with a secondary or higher education and those in the fourth wealth quintile were more likely to receive IPT during an ANC visit than other women (2015 NMIS).

Routine HMIS data over the last three years have shown improvements in the rate of IPTp uptake among pregnant women visiting the health facilities. Figure 6 below shows the proportion of ANC re-visits at which IPTp2 was received as reported through the national DHIS2 platform. This shows a general increase in the proportion of women who receive IPTp2 in PMI focus states.

Figure 6. Prevalence of IPTp2 in PMI-Focus States, 2012-2015

Prevalence of IPTp Second Dose in PMI Focus States, 2012-2015

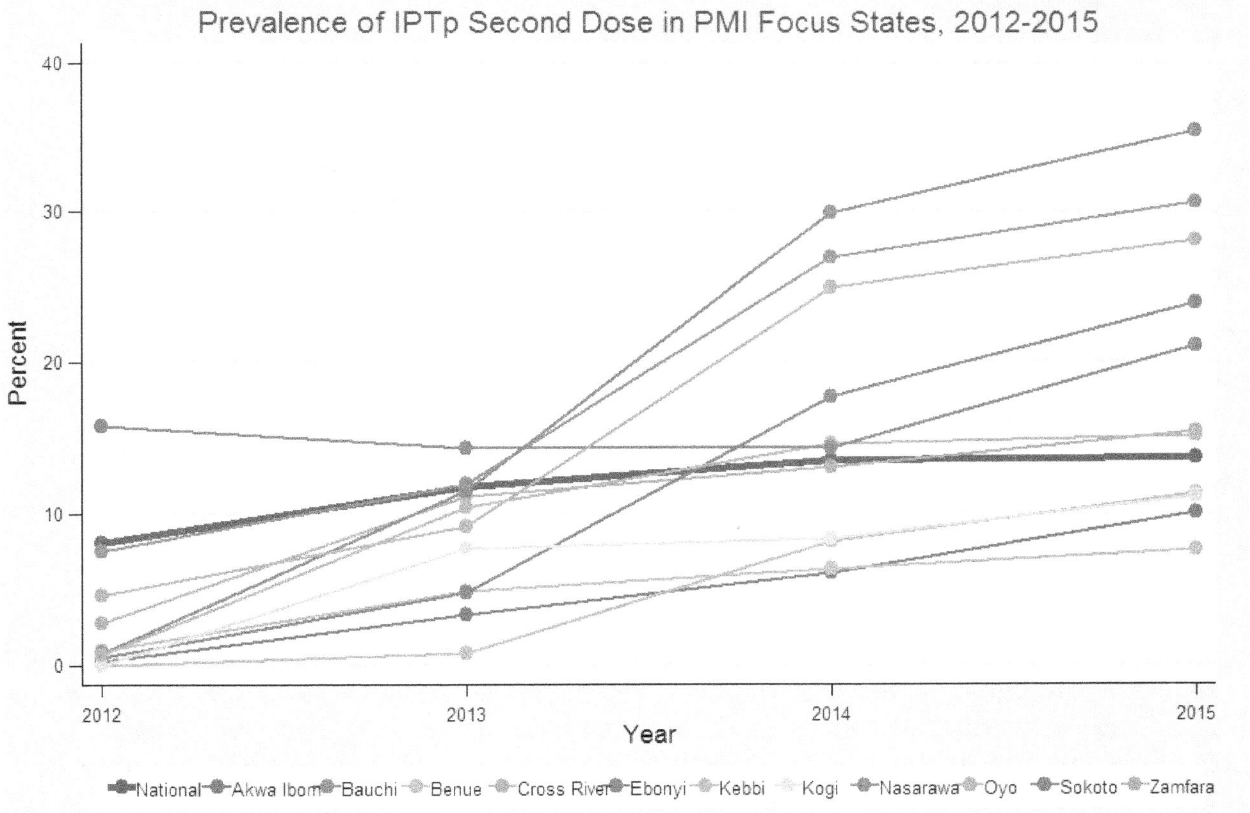

Although data show improvements in uptake, MIP outcome indicators are still low. Average ANC4+ attendance is 51% (2013 NDHS) while IPTp1 coverage is 47% and IPTp2 coverage is 37% (2015 MIS). As observed during field visits to some hospitals, non-pharmaceutical service providers are not allowed to dispense SP, as such, SP may not be available at ANC clinics. A combination of service delivery gaps result in missed opportunities for IPTp DOT, ITNs, and proper management of malaria for the pregnant women.

Progress during the past 12-18 months
In 2015, PMI supported the dissemination of the new IPTp guidelines of providing IPTp at every scheduled ANC visit after the first trimester, with four weeks between doses, and revised the quantification of SP to align with the new policy using three instead of two ANC visits, and updated the training materials and algorithms. The national dissemination of the new guideline took place in June 2015. State level dissemination was done in the 11 PMI-supported states. PMI and State Malaria Elimination Programs (SMEP) used the dissemination of the new IPTp guidelines as a catalyst to set up MIP TWGs, and strengthen the implementation of MIP activities in states. With FY 2015 funding, PMI procured 4 million SP doses and 2 million ITNs for routine distribution through health facilities.

Based on the new IPTp policy and guidelines, there was a need to increase the knowledge and capacity of health workers. PMI supported a rapid scale up of training of health workers specifically on the IPTp new policy. With FY 2015 funding, PMI trained over 3,098 ANC service providers on prevention and management of MIP. PMI continued to train all relevant health workers in the 11 PMI-supported states, irrespective of whether they work at PMI or Global Fund supported facilities. The HMIS reporting forms and the DHIS2 application are yet to be updated to allow reporting of additional IPTp doses beyond the IPTp2. There has been no evidence of training for private sector health workers by the government and other development partners in the country.

As observed during field visits to some hospitals, non-pharmaceutical service providers are not allowed to dispense SP, as such, SP may not be available at ANC clinics. A combination of service delivery gaps result in missed opportunities for IPTp DOT, ITNs, and proper management of malaria for the pregnant women. However, PMI is working with NMEP, the Pharmacy Council of Nigeria, the States, and other malaria partners to allow non-pharmaceutical health workers to stock and dispense SP at ANC clinics, and capture the data in the health facility HMIS.

In two northern states (Kebbi and Zamfara), PMI is supporting the implementation of routine outreach by facility-based health workers to provide a package of ANC services, including MIP interventions, to the communities where the health facility is located. This activity is being implemented in approximately 10 local government areas in each state. It is estimated that approximately 156,000 pregnant women will be reached and given IPTp through the outreach IPTp delivery channel over a period of 6 months.

Table 10: SP Gap Analysis for Malaria in Pregnancy (2016-2018)

Calendar Year	2016	2017	2018
Total Country Population	192,935,362	199,220,487	205,723,765
Total Targeted Population (11 PMI-supported states)	52,885,275	54,553,493	56,274,521
Population of Pregnant Women in PMI States[1]	2,644,264	2,727,675	2,813,726
Pregnant women attending ANC[2] (57%, 60%, and 63%)	1,507,230	1,636,605	1,772,647
Number of pregnant women attending public health facility for ANC[3] (60%, 62%, and 64%)	904,338	1,014,695	1,134,494
SP Need for Public Health Facility[4]	2,713,015	3,044,085	3,403,482
SP need for Outreach[5]	271,301	304.408	356,640
Total SP Treatment Need	**2,984,316**	**3,348,493**	**3,760,122**
Partner Contributions (For 11 PMI supported states)			
SP carried over from previous year	1,694,710	4,545,877	4,776,312
SP from Government	0	0	
SP from Global Fund	1,835,483	1,578,928	0
SP from Other Donors	0	0	0
SP planned with PMI funding	4,000,000	2,000,000	3,000,000
Total SP Available	**7,530,193**	**8,124,805**	**7,776,312**
Total SP Surplus (Gap)	4,545,877	4,776,312	4,016,190
SPs needed to fill the pipeline (10 months)	2,486,930	2,790,411	3,133,435

Assumptions:

[1] The expected number of pregnant women in Nigeria is 5% of the total population. Federal Government of Nigeria Official Gazette No 4, Lagos 19th January 2007 Vol 94. Page B 47-53.

[2] Calculated using state-specific ANC coverage by skilled provider - DHS 2013; estimated 3% increase per year.

[3] Calculated assuming that on average 60% of pregnant women seek care from public health facilities; estimated 2% increase per year.

[4] Calculated assuming every pregnant woman will receive 3 treatments of SP.

[5] Calculated assuming 10% of health facility SP-need will cater for women benefiting from health facility outreach.

Plans and Justification:

PMI strategy in Nigeria is to support NMEP and the 11 PMI focus states to raise IPTp coverage and minimize the missed opportunities among women who attend ANC in specific states. PMI will collaborate with other partners to advocate for the availability of low dose folic acid in the PMI focused states. Efforts will focus on increasing IPTp coverage through provision of free SP to pregnant women, implementing the WHO IPTp policy, expanding ITN distribution to pregnant women during the first ANC visit, and testing and promptly treating pregnant women with confirmed malaria. With FY 2017 funds, PMI will identify LGAs in three states (Sokoto, Kebbi, and Zamfara) to support health facility outreach for ANC services that include IPTp.

Proposed activities with FY 2017 funding ($2,340,000):

1. *Procure 3 million SP* treatments to support implementation of IPTp as part of FANC across the 11 PMI-supported states. *($540,000)*

2. *Capacity building and scale-up for MIP*: Strengthen capacity and integrated supportive supervision for MIP service delivery within the FANC platform in 11 PMI-supported states. Support includes in-service training, introducing new guidelines in medical training institutions and professional associations, expanding of IPTp in health facilities and through outreach services. Private sector health providers will benefit from training on IPTp during malaria case management training. *($1,800,000)*

3. *ITN continuous distribution channel*: PMI will support routine distribution of ITNs to pregnant women during the first ANC visit. *(Costs covered under the ITN section)*

4. *SBCC activities to promote IPTp and net use*: PMI will continue to promote ANC uptake among pregnant women through integrated activities that are outlined in the SBCC section of this MOP.

3. Case management

a. Diagnosis and treatment

NMEP/PMI objectives

The Nigerian National Guidelines for Diagnosis and Treatment of Malaria are aligned with the WHO recommendations on universal diagnostic testing and treatment with an artemisinin-based combination therapy (ACT). The NMSP 2014-2020 outlines Nigeria's priorities in the area of case management. The objectives for case management are:

- To test all care-seeking persons with suspected malaria using a rapid diagnostic test (RDT) or microscopy by 2020.

- To treat all individuals with confirmed malaria seen in public or private facilities with effective antimalarial drugs by 2020.

These objectives are to be achieved through the following strategies:

- Create demand for utilization of parasitological confirmation of malaria.
- Ensure availability of and access to equipment and supplies for parasitological confirmation of malaria, and commodities and supplies for treatment of uncomplicated and severe malaria.
- Build capacity of personnel for malaria case management in public and private health facilities, and at the community level through integrated community case management (iCCM).
- Strengthen capacity of public and private facilities for management of severe malaria.
- Implement a comprehensive national strategy for effective participation of the private sector in malaria case management.
- Strengthen systems for QA and QC of malaria diagnostic services.
- Conduct drug therapeutic efficacy testing (DTET).

The NMEP receives technical assistance and coordinates partners through the case management technical sub-committee. PMI is an active member and also assisted in the development of a diagnostic task force that reports to sub-committee.

Microscopy requires highly skilled staff. The NMEP considers secondary and tertiary hospitals, and large health centers with inpatient beds, as the facilities where microscopy should be available. The NMEP expects RDTs to be used at all facilities where microscopy is not available, to complement microscopy in secondary facilities, and in certain outpatient clinics of tertiary facilities. The target for parasitological diagnosis is 100% in the public sector and 80% in the private sector and community (where iCCM is implemented) by 2018.

Artemether-lumefantrine (AL) and artesunate-amodiaquine (ASAQ) are the two recommended first-line treatments of uncomplicated malaria in Nigeria, including for children weighing less than 5 kg with appropriate dosing. In 2012, the NMEP changed the first-line treatment of severe malaria from quinine to injectable artesunate (IAS), consistent with WHO treatment guidelines. The National Guideline for Diagnosis and Treatment of Malaria 2015 specifies that pregnant women with uncomplicated malaria should receive oral quinine + clindamycin in the first trimester and an ACT in the second and third trimesters, while severe malaria should be treated with IAS (or intravenous quinine, if IAS is not available). The recommended pre-referral treatment of severe malaria is intramuscular or rectal artesunate, intravenous quinine, or intravenous artemether. The target for malaria treatment is that 80% of persons with a parasite-based diagnosis of malaria will receive prompt antimalarial treatment according to the national treatment policy by 2017, and 100% by 2020.

The 2015 NMIS found that 66% of children under age five with fever were taken for advice or treatment; but only 30% were taken to a public health facility. Although the final 2015 NMIS report is pending, the 2010 NMIS found that 57% of household members first sought treatment for fever at a chemist's store or private patent medicine vendor (PPMV), including 56% of children under five years. Most PPMVs receive some informal on-the-job training as apprentices on the recognition of basic symptoms of uncomplicated malaria and are empowered to provide treatment.

The NMEP intends to expand access to malaria case management through iCCM. Although led by the Child Health Division, iCCM is an important component of national malaria policies. The target was to ensure that at least 80% of children under five living in selected communities had access to quality care through iCCM by 2015. This was not achieved due to a delay in starting and the challenge of commodities.

ICCM has been implemented in Nigeria since 2014, but has been implemented on a relatively small scale. The Canadian International Development Agency supports implementation of iCCM in two states (Abia and Niger) as part of the WHO Rapid Access Expansion (RACE) program in five countries including Nigeria. Intervention covers all LGAs in Abia and nine LGAs in Niger State. The Global Fund supports the rollout of the malaria component in the remaining 21 LGAs in Niger, while WHO funds the additional non-malaria commodities. ICF-International provides semi-annual data quality assessments to the project. A planned independent impact evaluation is to take place in December 2016. Currently, USAID-Nigeria, through maternal, neonatal and child health funding, is implementing national-level advocacy support to the Federal Ministry of Health, and landscaping the different models of community-level case management to determine a sustainable model for Nigeria. PMI-Nigeria will use lessons learned from the RACE iCCM project, landscape activity, and the PPMV/case management pilots to implement iCCM in PMI-supported states.

Community health workers do perform RDTs currently in health center settings. The results of the impact evaluation will inform expansion of this ability into the community setting away from health centers.

Following the WHO recommendation of SMC for children aged between 3 and 59 months in areas of highly seasonal malaria transmission across the Sahel sub-region, the NMEP included SMC in its new strategic plan. The NMEP strategy recommends SMC in nine states in the Sahel region: Sokoto, Kebbi, Zamfara, Bauchi, Katsina, Kano, Jigawa, Yobe, and Borno. This translates to 227 LGAs and a population of 10.9 million children under the age of five years. Within the three Sahelian states supported by PMI (Kebbi, Sokoto, and Zamfara), there are 2,815,505 children between 3-59 months of age (eligible for SMC) projected for 2018.

Progress since PMI was launched
Since PMI began in Nigeria, case management support has been directed at the following key areas: 1) procurement and distribution of diagnostic and treatment commodities; 2) training and supervision of laboratory and clinical care personnel in accurate malaria diagnostics and appropriate treatment; 3) implementation of QA systems for malaria diagnostics.

Since 2011, PMI has procured 21 million RDTs and distributed 17 million, including RDTs procured by other donors and distributed with PMI funds; procured 59 million ACTs and distributed 32 million; and procured and distributed 120,000 vials of IAS.

PMI has supported states in developing detailed training plans on case management (including diagnostics) that have incorporated input from each state's MoH, local health care institutions, development partners, and implementing partners. Each plan identified the number of facilities, the cadre of health workers to be trained, and the implementing partner responsible for training in a particular area. Because partners other than PMI (e.g. UNICEF, Global Fund) also supported this large-scale training initiative—often with many partners in the same state—activities were coordinated to avoid duplication. For each state, trainers (consisting of physicians, nurses, pharmacists, and laboratory scientists) were trained in the fundamentals of malaria case management. These trainers subsequently conducted training in LGAs throughout the state. Separate sessions targeted specific providers, ranging from community health workers to physicians. Microscopy training for laboratory technicians was also provided in each of the PMI focus states. Trainings were followed by on-the-job mentoring by trainers and project staff, and supportive supervision by the MoH staff.

By the end of FY 2015, PMI had supported the training of 10,288 health workers in malaria diagnostics (9,998 in RDT and 290 in microscopy) out of the 44,546 targeted (23%); and 14,746 health workers in treatment with ACTs at health facilities and in the community, out of the 39,040 targeted (50%). These trainings covered 17% and 38% of the health workers targeted by the states for diagnostics and treatment, respectively.

PMI has been a driving force behind the development of a malaria diagnostic QA system. In collaboration with the DoD-Walter Reed Program and other partners, PMI supported the NMEP in developing and finalizing a QA framework and the Malaria Diagnostic External Quality Assurance (EQA) Operational Guidelines for parasite-based confirmation of malaria in 2012. In 2013, before the QA documents were finalized, PMI began piloting the QA system in two supported states. In addition to supporting the operational guidelines, PMI assisted in creating supervisory tools, standard operating procedures (SoP), and work plans. Guidelines call for quarterly facility visits for lab supervision, slide validation, and on-the-job mentoring. During these on-site supervisory visits, evaluators and local microscopists read slides together and discuss discrepancies. PMI has now supported the roll out of EQA in all 11 PMI-supported states. A total of 90 QA officers have received training in malaria diagnostics and QA supervision. The trained QA officers were drawn from national and PMI-supported states.

Since the NMEP changed the first-line treatment of severe malaria in 2012, PMI has trained 359 senior health providers in clinical care of severe malaria using IAS. PMI has also procured 120,000 vials of IAS for use in PMI-supported states. With UNITAID funding, Malaria Consortium and Clinton Foundation Health Access Initiative (CHAI) have trained 645 health workers across the country to manage severe malaria with IAS. Medicines for Malaria Venture, Global Fund, and the GoN have also procured IAS.

NMEP policy supports the use of pre-referral rectal artesunate in suspected cases of severe malaria presenting to community health workers (CHWs) or peripheral health facilities. However, cultural and operational barriers—namely, poor referral linkages to the formal health system, limited availability of rectal artesunate, and poor supervision and reporting—have prevented the implementation of this activity.

The NMEP has established 14 sentinel sites throughout the country to monitor the efficacy of the first-line treatments. The sites utilize the WHO standardized protocol and are scheduled to conduct the studies biannually. Drug therapeutic efficacy testing (DTET) conducted in 2009/10 and published in 2014 demonstrated greater than 95% PCR-corrected cure rates at 28 days for both first-line ACTs.[5] In 2014, another DTET commenced, with final report still pending. Additional molecular analysis including K13 genotyping was conducted (results pending).

Progress during the past 12-18 months
In FY 2015, PMI ordered 6,718,000 RDTs and distributed 6,747,289 RDTs (from both PMI and Global Fund sources), and ordered 19,304,880 ACTs and distributed 18,412,586 ACTs to PMI- and Global Fund-supported health facilities in the 11 PMI-supported states. Case management training continued in FY 2015 with 6,886 health workers (1,524 at health facility and 5,342 CHWs) trained in case management with ACTs, and 2,262 trained in malaria laboratory diagnostics in the 11 PMI-supported states.

The 2015 NMIS reported that only 13% of children under five years with fever had blood taken for testing. While this denotes an increase from 5% (2010 NMIS), it is still very low. The end-use verification (EUV) survey and HMIS provides further background on Nigeria's progress in malaria case management at the health facility level in the public sector.

A PMI EUV survey was conducted in PMI-supported states in February 2016 assessing 110 health facilities. The survey showed stockout rates of 5% for RDTs and 6% for SP; 100% of facilities had some form of ACT available for treatment of malaria. Seventy-four percent of fever cases were diagnosed as malaria, with 31% under age five years. Of those children diagnosed with malaria, 81% were diagnosed by RDT and 4% by microscopy, and 83% were treated with an ACT.

According to HMIS reports the national confirmation rate (by microscopy and RDTs) for uncomplicated malaria cases in public health facilities increased from 51% in 2014 to 56% in 2015. Figure 7 shows that the confirmation rate for PMI-supported states increased from 61% (2014) to 67% (2015), ranging from a low of 48% in Sokoto to a high of 94% in Ebonyi in 2015. Although the increase is modest, most of the PMI-supported states show an increasing trend in

---

[5] Oguche S, Okafor HU, Watila I, Meremikwu M, Agomo P, Ogala W, et al. Efficacy of artemisinin-based combination treatments of uncomplicated falciparum malaria in under-five year-old Nigerian children. Am J Trop Med Hyg. 2014; 91:925–935. doi: 10.4269/ajtmh.13-0248

malaria testing except the two northern states of Bauchi and Sokoto. PMI/Nigeria is investigating the lack of progress in those two states.

Figure 7. Percentage of all reported fever cases confirmed by a malaria diagnostic test (confirmation rate) for uncomplicated malaria cases reported through the HMIS, by PMI-Nigeria focus state: 2014-2015

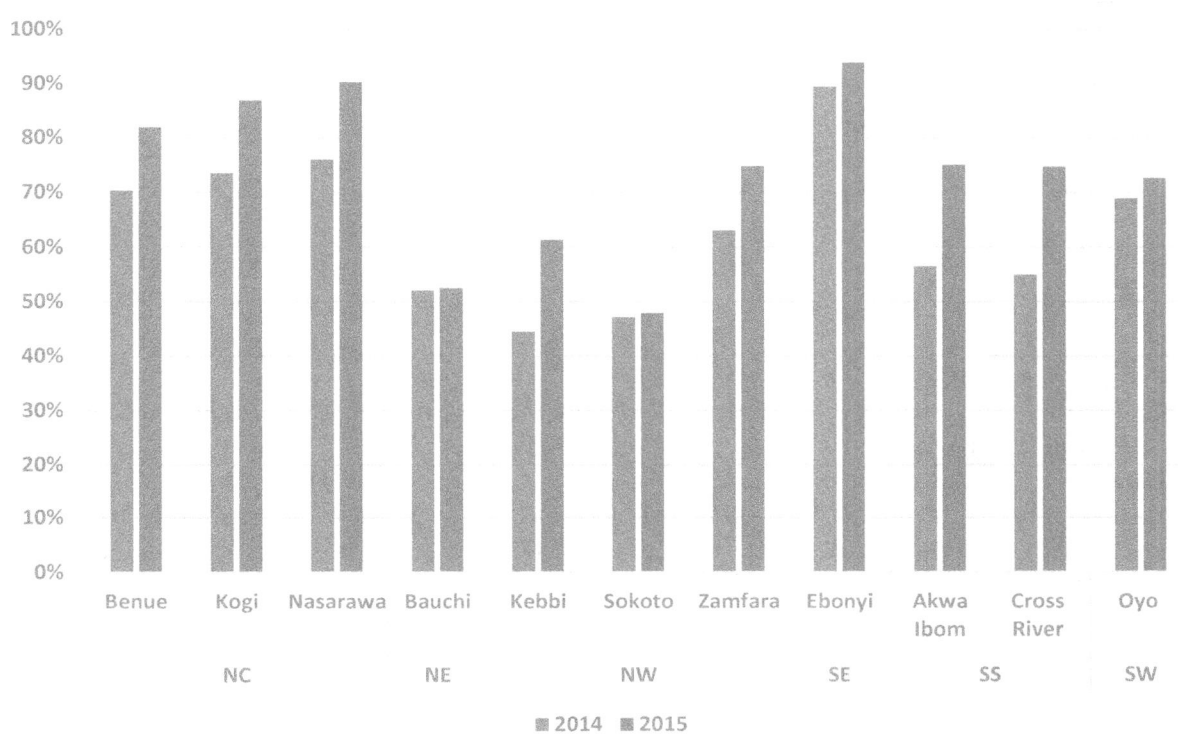

PMI continued to support malaria diagnostic QA. In 2015, two EQA visits occurred in each of seven PMI-supported states. Public sector health worker strikes and logistic challenges prevented the conduct of quarterly EQA in these seven states. External QA systems are in development in two additional states. Key findings from the EQA visits were absence of SOPs, inadequate documentation, lack of basic consumables and equipment, and poor storage conditions for RDTs. QA capacity was further strengthened through WHO certification of two Level 1 and nine Level 2 expert microscopists trained in country. These expert microscopists serve as trainers, constitute the core of the QA program, and provide support for malaria research including DTET.

Private sector integrated community case management
The National Guideline for iCCM, approved in 2013, clearly states the importance of iCCM to increase access to effective management of childhood illnesses. In January 2015, the Pharmacists Council of Nigeria approved registered PPMVs and community pharmacists to carry out RDTs

57

before providing antimalarial drugs. In order to effectively reach the large percentage of Nigerians who seek malaria care in the private sector, PMI is supporting a pilot study of PPMVs in two LGAs in Ebonyi State. The study has intervention and control arms focusing on PPMVs and their corresponding catchment areas. The baseline data shows that caregivers' top two preferences for seeking treatment of childhood illnesses were a PPMV (40%) and a public health facility (23%).[6] Because PPMVs could not legally diagnose or treat malaria until recently, case management had occurred mostly unrecorded and unregulated in this sector. The baseline evaluation also revealed that two-thirds of PPMVs had never heard of nor seen a malaria-RDT. The end-line report for this pilot is expected December 2016.

A Global Fund supported pilot study of malaria RDT feasibility and use among Nigerian PPMVs, completed in June 2014, showed that more than 90% of the PPMVs adhered to correct RDT techniques. The pilot sought to increase testing and treatment among PPMVs as first points of contact, strengthen the quality of diagnosis and treatment and maintain it, and promote the use of these services to caregivers in the community. An end-line evaluation will occur in August 2016.

Seasonal malaria chemoprevention (SMC)
To date, PMI/Nigeria has not supported SMC given other program priorities. Funding from other donors including DfID, Dangote Foundation, and UNITAID, Malaria Consortium, and CHAI has supported SMC in Jigawa, Katsina, Kano, Sokoto and Zamfara states. The only ongoing SMC is funded by UNITAID, implemented by Malaria Consortium, began in 2015, supports 17 LGAs in two states (Sokoto and Zamfara), and is targeting 800,000 children. The HMIS shows that the supported LGAs are reporting a decrease in malaria cases among the target population.

---

[6] (USAID/MalariaCare Project, February 2016): *Improved Community Case management of Childhood Illnesses by patent Proprietary Medicine Vendors: Baseline Evaluation Report*

Commodity gap analysis

Table 11: RDT Gap Analysis (2016-2018)

Calendar year	2016	2017	2018
RDT needs			
Total country population	192,935,362	199,220,487	205,723,765
Population at risk for malaria (97%)[a]	187,147,302	193,243,873	199,552,052
PMI targeted population (11 PMI-supported states)	52,885,275	54,553,493	56,274,521
Total number of projected fever cases[b]	89,904,967	92,740,939	95,666,686
Percent of fever cases tested with RDT (public sector)[c]	84%	84%	84%
Total RDT needs[d, e, f]	10,784,281	15,099,602	20,026,230
Partner contributions			
RDTs carried over from previous year	5,751,921	3,267,640	4,468,039
RDTs from government	0	0	0
RDTs from Global Fund[g]	6,300,000	6,300,000	6,300,000
RDTs from other donors	0	0	0
RDTs planned with PMI funding	2,000,000	10,000,000	16,562,500
Total RDTs available	14,051,921	19,567,640	27,330,539
Total Annual RDT surplus (gap)	**3,267,640**	**4,468,039**	**7,304,309**
Pipeline need (6 months)	5,392,140	7,549,801	10,013,115

Assumptions:
(a) 97% of the total population is at risk of malaria.
(b) Projected fever cases estimated at an average of 1.7 fevers per person per year in PMI focus states.
(c) Average 84% RDT use (HMIS)
(d) Average 68% care seeking for fever, with 30% public sector (2015 MIS), then increasing by five percentage points per year. Public sector includes both PMI-supported and non-supported health centers.
(e) Diagnostic testing rates of 70 (2016), 80 (2017), and 90 (2018) percent (consensus estimate)
(f) Additional 5% of fever cases tested in public sector will be managed at the community level (iCCM) in Zamfara, Sokoto, Bauchi and Kebbi states. (equivalent to addition an additional 1.8% of public sector RDTs)
(g) Global Fund will procure the same number of RDTs as in 2016

Table 12: ACT Gap Analysis (2016-2018)

Calendar year	2016	2017	2018
ACT needs			
Total country population	192,935,362	199,220,487	205,723,765
Population at risk for malaria[a]	187,147,302	193,243,873	199,552,052
PMI targeted population (11 PMI-supported states)	52,885,275	54,553,493	56,274,521
Projected number of malaria cases (public sector) [b-e]	12,655,023	14,259,306	15,515,109
Total ACT needs (public sector)[f, g]	14,360,700	15,848,514	16,581,984
Partner contributions			
ACTs carried over from previous year	20,436,096	17,661,751	10,713,236
ACTs from government	0	0	0
ACTs from Global Fund (directed toward PMI focus states)	2,900,000	2,900,000	2,900,000
ACTs from other donors	0	0	0
ACTs planned with PMI funding	8,686,355	6,000,000	3,000,000
Total ACTs available	32,022,451	26,561,751	16,613,236
Total Annual ACT surplus (gap)	17,661,751	10,713,236	31,253
Pipeline need (6 months)	7,180,350	7,924,257	8,290,992

Assumptions:
(a) 97% of total population is at risk of malaria.
(b) Projected fever cases are estimated at an average of 1.7 fevers per person per year in PMI focus states.
(c) Average of 68% care seeking for fever, with 30% in public sector (2015 MIS), then increasing by five percentage points per year. Public sector includes both PMI-supported and non-supported health centers.
(d) Diagnostic testing rates of 70 (2016), 80 (2017), and 90(2018) percent (consensus estimate)
(e) Test positivity rate would decrease from 69% (HMIS data) in 2016 to 64% in 2017 and 59% in 2018.
(f) All those not tested will be presumptively treated with an ACT.
(g) Additional cases will be treated with ACTs through iCCM in Zamfara, Sokoto, Bauchi, and Kebbi states (133,006 in 2017 and 162,519 in 2018).

Quantification of IAS for the treatment of severe malaria is estimated on the assumption that 5% of all malaria cases will be severe and—averaging the amount required for the different ages and treatment durations—that a case will require 5.5 ampules for a full treatment course. For 2018, the total need for IAS at public health facilities is estimated to be 4.2 million vials based on approximately 5% of 15.5 million malaria cases (775,000) being referred from the community or health facility in PMI-supported states.

Plans and justification

In FY 2017, PMI will build on the progress to date in strengthening case management, through the scale-up of malaria diagnostic testing, appropriate treatment, and QA systems. PMI will continue to support the NMEP's malaria case management policy through provision of malaria commodities, case management training/refresher training, supportive supervision, and diagnostic QA/QC.

PMI supports national and state level malaria commodity quantification exercises to improve the accuracy of RDT and ACT forecasts. PMI expects the RDT need will continue to increase as case management implementation and iCCM expand. PMI will procure and distribute approximately 16.5 million RDTs and 3 million ACTs to help meet the projected need in PMI supported states. In addition, PMI will procure microscopy supplies. Historically, the priority for commodity distribution was the health facilities where PMI had conducted training of health workers and was supporting on-the-job training and supervision. Other facilities received commodities based on availability and need, especially in support of the vision of the Nigerian MoH of at least one well-performing health facility per ward. Going forward, PMI will continue to work with other donors and the state governments to more effectively pool supplies to ensure that all facilities in PMI supported states will experience a smoother supply chain with fewer stockouts.

PMI will build on its experience and progress to date to further improve case management practices. A core component of this will be the on-the-job training and supervision of health care providers to continue to improve capacity at the community, facility, and state levels. This ongoing support will strengthen diagnostic and treatment services at all levels of the health care system by identifying areas that require improvement and providing on-site feedback and technical advice.

PMI will begin to use routine malaria data reported through the DHIS2 system to monitor case management performance at the health facility level (e.g. stockouts, percentage of malaria cases confirmed, over-prescription of ACTs, etc.). At the state level, PMI's implementing partners will assist LGAs in using HMIS to monitor health facility case management performance (confirmation rates, ACT treatments) to complement supportive supervision and direct efforts to where they are most needed. Based on performance, the routine quarterly supervision visits will be adjusted so that well-functioning health facilities would require fewer visits, and lower performing facilities might need visits more than quarterly. In addition, the PMI country team currently uses DHIS2 on a semiannual basis to make programmatic decisions, to monitor implementing partner performance, and to inform the portfolio review, annual report to Congress, and MOP planning.

PMI will also support the strengthening of QA for malaria diagnostics. This support will assist in the implementation of the Malaria Diagnostic External Quality Assurance Operational Guidelines that includes both microscopy and RDTs in PMI-supported states. This activity is closely linked with the on-the-job training and supervision of health care providers at the facility

61

level. In-country QA lot testing also takes place on RDTs in use throughout the country. These QA activities are expected to build confidence in RDT results among health care providers.

PMI Nigeria will plan to gradually expand the private sector activities with PPMVs that began as a pilot in Ebonyi. Results from the pilot will be available by the end of 2016, and lessons learned will be applied moving forward. A key issue for sustainability is supervision. PMI will explore regulatory mechanisms with the Pharmacists Council of Nigeria as well as PPMV associations as possible structures for supervision and enforcement.

With the 2015 NMIS showing persistently high parasitemia in the North West Zone despite high levels of ITN ownership and use, PMI plans to add support to SMC efforts targeted at children under the age of five years. PMI will build upon iCCM activities already supported and procure drugs recommended for SMC (SP plus AQ). Since ASAQ is one of Nigeria's first-line treatments, PMI will work with the NMEP and states to make sure that AL is the deployed ACT used in the SMC areas. The procurement of ASAQ has already been markedly reduced nationally due to provider and patient preferences. PMI will also make adjustments at the state level for the slight increase in RDT and ACT needs during SMC. For FY 2017, PMI proposes to cover 15% of the SMC-eligible children in the three Sahelian states it currently supports (Kebbi, Sokoto, and Zamfara). The estimated target is thus 422,326 children between 3-59 months of age, receiving four doses of SP-AQ at monthly intervals over the 4-month malaria transmission season at a total estimated cost per child of $3.00.

PMI will continue to support DTET to monitor efficacy of first-line antimalarial drugs including K-13 analysis.

PMI will support SBCC to increase patient awareness and demand for appropriate testing and treatment through media and community level activities, as well as to improve health care provider adherence to case management guidelines through activities directed at health facilities (see description in the SBCC section).

Proposed activities with FY 2017 funding ($21,925,000)

1. *Procure RDTs and microscopy supplies:* Procure about 16.5 million RDTs to fill gaps and help prevent stockouts of malaria diagnostic tests in the public sector in 11 PMI-supported states. *($5,300,000)*

2. *Strengthen malaria diagnosis, including QA/QC system:* Conduct training of trainers for malaria diagnostics QA; conduct EQA visits in 11 states; and support a state reference laboratory for malaria diagnostics QA/QC.

3. *Procure ACTs:* Procure 3 million ACTs to fill gaps and help prevent stockouts of antimalarial medications in the public sector in 11 PMI-supported states. *($2,580,000)*

4. *Procure sulfadoxine/pyrimethamine plus amodiaquine (SP+AQ):* Procure 1,689,300 treatments of SP+AQ for SMC in several LGAs in the states of Kebbi, Sokoto, and Zamfara. *($850,000)*

5. *Build capacity, and strengthen service delivery for case management at public health facilities (including iCCM):* Refresher training of health care workers in approximately 5,000 health facilities at all levels on malaria case management; training/refresher training of laboratory staff in malaria diagnosis (RDT and microscopy); trainer of trainers on diagnostics QA; support states to conduct supportive supervision and on-the-job capacity building; and providing basic tools and job aids for malaria case management. *($10,465,250) [$9,965,250 for nine states, and $500,000 for two states of Sokoto and Bauchi where PMI expects to leverage additional funds from other integrated primary care interventions funding mechanisms).*

   Specifically, the activities to be conducted in each state will include:
   i. Train/refresh the different categories of health workers in approximately 5,000 health facilities on case management in the public sector in PMI supported states *($4,160,250)*.
   ii. Conduct on-the-job training and supportive supervision for staff in approximately 5,000 health facilities in PMI-supported states *($4,000,000)*.
   iii. Provide basic tools such as printed or on-line guidelines and job aids in the form of guideline summaries and wall charts for rapid reference on the job, for malaria case management in approximately 5,000 health facilities *($500,000)*.
   iv. Train and supervise community health workers in 230 LGAs in all aspects of malaria case management *($1,805,000)*.

6. *Capacity building for malaria case management in the private sector:* Provide PPMVs with iCCM training with special emphasis on RDT use to expand quality care in the private sector; work with regulatory mechanisms to support PPMV supervision; and explore options for low cost, quality RDTs for the private sector. *($841,000)*

7. *DTET:* Support DTET in five sentinel sites at a cost of $60,000/site to monitor efficacy of first-line antimalarial drugs. This will include the K-13 analysis. *($300,000)*

8. *SMC implementation:* Implementation of SMC for all LGAs in three states, including microplanning, training, drug administration, supervision, monitoring, and reporting, for approximately 423,000 children. Costs for advocacy and creating demand for SMC are under SBCC section. *($1,268,750 [$951,750 for two states of Kebbi and Zamfara, and $317,000 for Sokoto state])*

9. *Technical assistance:* Two CDC technical visits to provide technical support for malaria diagnostics and QA. *($20,000)*

b. Pharmaceutical management

NMEP/PMI objectives

The NMSP 2014-2020 objective is to ensure the timely availability of appropriate antimalarial medicines and commodities required for prevention and treatment of malaria in Nigeria wherever they are needed by 2018, through the following strategies:

1) Strengthen procurement-related processes.
2) Develop efficient distribution systems for antimalarial medicines and commodities (storage, transport distribution, and inventory management).
3) Strengthen logistics management.
4) Implement policies on QA and pharmacovigilance.
5) Operationalize and update where necessary existing policies for malaria case management in the private sector.
6) Increase access to antimalarial prevention and management commodities in the private sector.
7) Strengthen collaboration with the National Agency for Food and Drug Administration and Control (NAFDAC) to put in place regulatory requirements for distribution including storage and transportation of antimalarial products in the private sector.

Health commodities management in the public sector is weak and fragmented. The frequent stockouts of all commodities, including ACTs and RDTs, occur at all levels, and negatively affects the quality of care given at public health facilities. NMEP and states programs recognize the chronic supply issues; hence pharmaceutical management is the fifth objective of the NMSP 2014-2020.

Commodities for management of malaria cases come from a various sources. They may be donated or procured at various levels of the government health system. Donors, the federal government, states, and LGAs all can procure ITNs, ACTs, SP, and RDTs. The states, LGAs, and individual health facilities can supplement donated and federal government-procured commodities by using revolving drug funds and/or revenues. Due to the multiple sources of malaria medicines in Nigeria, it is critical that the NAFDAC and federal and state ministries of health address issues surrounding quality of medicines to combat counterfeit and substandard quality drugs.

Distribution systems of commodities vary. Essential medicines procured by donors and government flow either through the Federal Medical Stores or the state central medical store (CMS). States often have difficulties delivering commodities to the facility level. The distribution of Global Fund- and other donor-procured ACTs experiences challenges at times, resulting in stockouts in some health facilities. This has led facilities to acquire medicines from local pharmacies that may not meet the required quality. More than half of all Nigerians use the private sector and local pharmacies for health care.

The NAFDAC is responsible for the registration of medicines. The agency is also responsible for QC of antimalarials at the point of entry for internationally procured drugs or at the factory gate for locally produced ones. Although Nigeria has almost 40 registered ACTs that are manufactured in Nigeria, to date, there is no producer that is WHO-prequalified. Additionally, products from nonqualified foreign manufacturers, as well as artemisinin monotherapies, SP, and chloroquine exist in the private sector. Given the scope and size of the private sector market and its common use by many Nigerians, NAFDAC has a difficult task providing quality control measures in this sector. NAFDAC and the NMEP collaborate to conduct post-marketing surveillance of malaria medicines. Before the accreditation of the NAFDAC laboratory, there was no WHO prequalified QC laboratory in Nigeria, so the NMEP had to send Global Fund-procured medicines to outside laboratories for testing.

Progress since PMI was launched
Despite the numerous challenges, opportunities have emerged to help improve some of the problems facing Nigeria's health commodity management. PMI funding has helped the GoN establish a malaria commodities logistics system for distribution of malaria commodities that include ACTs, RDTs, SP, IAS, and ITNs. The support includes quantification and procurement planning, procuring and storage of commodities, distribution to states and health facilities or communities in the case of ITNs for mass campaigns, and EUV surveys to monitor stock levels and prevent stockouts, excesses, and leakage.

PMI funding has supported the establishment of a logistics management information system (LMIS) in the 11 PMI-supported states. The LMIS generates data for quantification and procurement planning, and effective management of malaria commodities to prevent excesses and expiries. PMI funding is also used to train health workers in the LMIS and the malaria commodities logistics system. PMI does not support every health facility in every state, thus, the LMIS has not been rolled out to every facility. The LMIS does assist with RDT and ACT forecasting, but cannot yet be relied upon alone.

PMI continues to assist the national and state malaria elimination programs on pharmaceutical supply management working groups in all the 11 PMI-supported states. As a result, state-specific quantifications and gap analyses have been developed and used to inform commodity planning by partners and as advocacy tools for resource mobilization. All PMI-supported states currently report consumption data for decision-making. Such data help state and national malaria control staff to conduct more accurate forecasting and quantification, and are used to advocate with local governments for support with commodities procurement and management. Still, there remains a need to focus on improving data quality.

Many PMI-supported states lack sufficient storage space and, in some cases, have no warehouses capable of storing malaria commodities according to standard pharmaceutical guidelines (i.e., ample space, acceptable storage conditions and standard storage procedures, explicit QA mechanisms, and adequate product security). Despite these challenges, PMI-supported facilities have been appropriately stocked, including through *ad hoc* redistribution of stocks between states, as needed. PMI continues to lease on average 165 pallet positions in a pharmaceutically-compliant store in Abuja. Some state governments have provided storage space for malaria commodities but of all the PMI-supported states, only Cross River and Sokoto have pharmaceutically-compliant stores. While access will improve with inputs from PMI and other partners, the need for trained personnel in warehouse management will continue, and is being addressed. PMI advocates to FMoH and states to commit to improving the commodities logistics systems, and reduce stockouts across all states.

In four states—Ebonyi, Bauchi, Sokoto, and Zamfara—PMI supports distribution of malaria commodities using a direct delivery and information capture (DDIC) system. This is a direct delivery of commodities from the state CMS to facilities via trucks. At the time of delivery, a trained State MoH staff member on the truck checks the facility's stock, determines need using an inventory control software package, and immediately provides the needed commodities. This model is designed to be an informed push or vendor-managed inventory system that is based on regular data collection, bimonthly distribution, and real-time reporting. The goal is to enhance effective distribution of commodities with real-time logistics data collection for decision-making. Importantly, DDIC frees health facilities' staff time to concentrate on their core clinical duties, and has reduced stockout rates below 5% for commodities in full supply. The remaining seven PMI-supported states operate a pull inventory control system where health facilities are resupplied after submission of logistics data. Although there has not yet been an independent evaluation of DDIC, PMI plans to evaluate the various last-mile distribution options. However, this direct delivery might not be appropriate or affordable in some states. Thus, PMI can work with state LMCUs and share best practices from other states. Only one of the states (Zamfara) has adopted the informed push system.

PMI also supports the strengthening of QA/QC of antimalarials. A gap analysis of the QA/QC of medicines was conducted to help support NAFDAC and the NMEP in developing a QA/QC policy for antimalarial medicines and diagnostics. The QA/QC policy document, stipulating the roles and responsibilities of the various government procurement and regulatory agencies, has now been finalized and approved by the national council on health. In addition, PMI supported the procurement of basic equipment including Minilabs® and consumables for monitoring quality of antimalarial medicines.

Progress during the past 12-18 months
PMI FY 2015 funding contributed to strengthening the malaria commodities logistics system and the LMIS through training and tools for data collection. PMI supported the establishment and operations of the Logistics Management Coordination Units (LMCUs) in all 11 PMI-supported states. The setup of LMCUs within the Directorate of Pharmaceutical Services, in the state MoH is at various levels of operationalization. The LMCU is comprised of state employees and logistics management advisors from the implementing partners in the states. Employees of the state lead the LMCUs. The LMCUs carry out all logistics activities (forecasting, supply plan, budgeting, pipeline monitoring, monitoring and supportive supervision, distribution plans and activities, inventory management, and stock status analysis) within the state. They harmonize and foster collaborations across the health commodities supply chain systems in the states, and build capacity of local government and health facilities

personnel in supply chain and logistics management. LMCUs have remained integral to reinforce and improve supply chain management best practices at the health facility level.

PMI is part of the Development Partners Group for Health (DPGH) supply chain TWG at the national level aimed at enhancing effective coordination of supply chain activities in the country. PMI supported and participated in the national forecast for malaria commodities 2015-2020. The forecast identified the malaria commodities needs and gaps for each state and the national summaries.

PMI supported the training of 2,430 state-level officers in basic supply chain management and on the malaria commodities logistics system. PMI FY 2015 funding supported two rounds of EUV surveys in 110 health facilities in 11 PMI-supported states. The most recent EUV survey in February 2016 shows that of those surveyed, 58% of health facility staff were trained in stock management. Through these trainings, PMI expects a cascading effect in which non-PMI supported health facilities will experience indirect benefits from this capacity building.

PMI funding supported the expansion of distribution of ACTs, RDTs, and SP from 3,306 to 3,722 health facilities, including 643 Global Fund-supported health facilities in the 11 PMI-supported states. PMI has taken over the distribution of malaria commodities to all health facilities previously supported by the Global Fund in Ebonyi and Nasarawa states. In the last 18 months, PMI supported the distribution of more than 22.8 million ACTs, 13.2 million RDTs, 11.6 million SP treatments, 9.0 million nets and 40,000 vials of IAS.

PMI support for improved QA/QC of antimalarial medicines includes training staff to strengthen the regulatory capacity of NAFDAC. A total of 65 staff members were trained on different aspects of QA/QC. PMI supported the ISO 17025 accreditation of the Central Quality Control Laboratory of NAFDAC in Oshodi, Lagos in 2015. PMI supported the maintenance of the ISO 17025 accreditation in 2016, which was communicated to NAFDAC management on March 10, 2016. PMI has also commenced the ISO 17025 accreditation process of two NAFDAC zonal QC laboratories in Agulu and Kaduna. This will reduce the workload on the central QC laboratory that carries out QA/QC for medicines produced by Nigerian manufacturers and imported into the country. NAFDAC is being empowered to carry out QA/QC activities for local manufacturers and importers of medicines to sustain the accreditation for subsequent years. This will improve QA/QC and encourage laboratory QC of medicines to assist in identification of substandard and counterfeit medicines. The country needs appropriate equipment and the right personnel to move NAFDAC toward meeting WHO standards for prequalification. The agency needs support at the various laboratories in the six geopolitical zones to strengthen QA/QC and post-marketing surveillance of medicines in the country.

Plans and justification
With the numerous challenges of disjointed procurement, supply, and distribution system, PMI remains committed to strengthening pharmaceutical and commodity management systems at the state, health facility, and community levels. FY 2017 funds will be used to support states to

move from paper-based to electronic databases. The support will include establishment of warehouse management software to complement the electronic LMIS for better supply chain management and stock analysis. PMI looks to further integrate the LMIS and DHIS2 for better data for decision-making and forecasting needs at the facility level. PMI funding will also be used to increase the proportion of health facilities benefiting from PMI support within the 11 PMI-supported states, using the most cost-effective and state-owned systems for commodity storage and distribution. Efforts will be made to advocate for integrated state logistics management systems with other donors and programs, particularly with the Global Fund. PMI will continue to look at possibilities to pool malaria commodities at state level in order to lessen the procurement-related supply shortages seen in non-PMI supported facilities. PMI will continue to strengthen states' capacity to manage PSM activities through the LMCU.

PMI will continue building the capacity of the government to conduct logistics monitoring and supervisory visits for post-distribution verification. EUV surveys will be carried out twice a year as currently supported by PMI. PMI funding will continue to support training of facility staff on the LMIS and provide technical assistance to support it becoming fully operational. In this way, facilities and states will improve their ability to generate reliable data on consumption, supply, needs, and distribution of pharmaceuticals and commodities.

Proposed activities with FY 2016 funding ($5,000,000)
1. *Strengthen the pharmaceutical and commodity management system* by:
    a. Strengthening the LMIS for better forecasting and management;
    b. Conduct EUVs in PMI-supported states twice a year;
    c. Improving distribution of pharmaceuticals, RDTs, and ITNs to mitigate the risk of stockouts of malaria commodities; and
    d. Providing proper warehousing, where needed, of malaria commodities to reduce the risk of expired drugs. *($4,000,000)*

2. *Provide support to strengthen NAFDAC's capacity:* Strengthen NAFDAC's capacity for drug QC including the procurement of necessary equipment and supplies. Support will include expanding the use of Minilabs® to perform key tests for drug quality in the field. Activities include post-market surveillance in priority states to detect counterfeit antimalarial drugs and use of monotherapies in the public and private sectors. The support will also include technical assistance for upgrading two additional NAFDAC regional laboratories and maintenance of the Lagos QC laboratory. *($1,000,000)*

4. Health system strengthening and capacity building

PMI supports a broad array of health system strengthening activities that cut across intervention areas, such as training of health workers, supply chain management, HMIS strengthening, drug quality monitoring, and capacity building for NMEP, states, and LGAs. Currently, the capacity building activities are limited to only the public sector and the private not-for-profit health facilities. PMI is helping to build entomologic capacity by supporting entomology trainings and implementation of entomology monitoring system, including insecticide resistance monitoring.

NMEP/PMI objectives

The main objective for health system strengthening under the NMSP 2014-2020 is captured under the program management objective. The overall objective is strengthening governance and coordination of stakeholders for effective program implementation. The six strategies for accomplishing this objective are:

- Build capacity at national, state, and LGA levels to deliver malaria control/elimination interventions
- Strengthen program coordination at national and sub-national levels
- Improve unified annual operational planning
- Strengthen malaria resource mobilization and financial management mechanisms
- Develop a comprehensive strategy for private sector engagement
- Strengthen timely reporting of malaria control activities at all levels and promote dissemination of all reports to relevant stakeholders.

To support these strategies, PMI, WHO, and the Global Fund provide assistance to the national, state, and LGA malaria programs; strengthen program management; and provide operational and technical guidance through training, supervision, and coordination meetings. The DfID-funded SuNMaP project provided day-to-day capacity building to NMEP and ten states; however, the program ended in March 2016. DfID is now designing a follow-on program that is expected to be in place by the end of 2016. The DfID-supported states will not overlap with the 11 PMI focus states of Cross River, Zamfara, Nasarawa, Sokoto, Bauchi, Benue, Ebonyi, Oyo, and Kogi, Akwa Ibom and Kebbi.

PMI and other development partners participate in various national-level technical and program management working groups, which develop policy, strategic documents, implementation guidelines, SOPs, as well as provide operational and scientific guidance. Because Nigeria is operating a federal system, PMI and other partners have paid special attention to the state and LGA levels for strengthening malaria program management, technical expertise, and surveillance, monitoring and evaluation (SM&E) capacity.

Progress since PMI was launched

From its inception in Nigeria, PMI has supported a variety of capacity building activities to improve delivery of malaria interventions through health facilities and, more recently, at the community level through PPMVs and CHWs. Specifically, PMI has supported short-term training and technical assistance to the NMEP; trained health workers at various service delivery points; and engaged in improving routine monitoring and data collection at state and LGA levels. The training of health workers includes modules on malaria diagnosis using RDTs and microscopy, treatment of uncomplicated and severe malaria, prevention of MIP, SBCC, program management, and SM&E, including HMIS and DHIS2. Capacity building includes providing supportive supervision and mentorship from NMEP to the states, from the states to the LGAs, from LGAs to the health facilities, from the health facilities to the community. The program management capacity building includes providing mentorship and supportive supervision within the different service delivery points in the health facility. Since 2011, PMI has supported training of 2,862 health facility in-charges in program management. PMI support also included production and distribution of job aids and SOPs to health facilities.

In the 11 PMI-supported states, PMI has strengthened the management and planning for the SMEP staff. PMI has supported SMEP staff to develop state malaria implementation guidelines, annual costed work plans, and training and supervision plans. At the national level, PMI has supported NMEP to review malaria control policies and strategic plans, to develop implementation guidelines, to design systems for supportive supervision and training, and to develop the capacity for commodity forecasting, quantification, procurement planning, and commodity logistics management. PMI has worked with other development partners to develop capacities for data collection through routine health information systems and data use.

Using the Office of the U.S. Global AIDS Coordinator funds, PMI has continued its support to strengthening of the NMEP's management capacity through assigning an SM&E specialist and logistician at NMEP, and SM&E officers in six PMI-supported states. The long-term technical assistance provider for logistics has developed the capacity of NMEP PSM to forecast and quantify commodities for Global Fund. They also developed procedures for third party logistics for distribution of Global Fund procured commodities from the Lagos national warehouse to the states; and from the states to the service delivery points. The long-term technical assistance providers have participated in developing the concept papers for the Global Fund malaria grant.

Through its Abuja-based resident advisors, local senior program experts and partners, PMI has provided significant on-the-job management and technical support to all government levels. In addition to supporting the working groups, the PMI team has worked closely with the NMEP to develop Global Fund concept notes, provide technical guidance for all PMI-supported malaria interventions, advise the NMEP on disseminating such guidance to the state and local levels, and develop the protocols for PMI-funded surveys such as the NMIS, and OR studies.

Since its inception in 2008, the Nigeria Field Epidemiology and Laboratory Training Program (NFELTP) has recruited 8 successive cohorts of trainees (residents) for a total of 318. The latest cohort was recruited in February 2016 with a total of 56 residents. Six cohorts have successfully completed the two-year training. Of the 318 residents that have gone through the program 44 (14%) have been supported through PMI funding. All 25 malaria residents currently in training have been posted to malaria programs in the states for their current or upcoming field assignments.

In September 2013, a NFELTP scientific seminar was held in Abuja, entitled "Strengthening NFELTP Malaria-Related Research," in order to develop malaria-related research projects to address identified gaps in NMEP research needs. Participants created an inventory of relevant research projects that they could implement and drafted research proposals on those topics. These were developed in line with the prioritized NMEP OR list. A second NFELTP scientific seminar was held at the end of May 2016.

Graduates of the program are now supporting NMEP (2 graduates), university (1), state commissioner (1), state malaria coordinators (1), while 13 are state epidemiologists. To date, NFELTP trainees have worked on 23 research projects that include case management (5), MIP (7), ITNs/IRS (7), and laboratory/diagnostics (4). Seventeen of the research projects are completed and some have been published.

Progress during the past 12-18 months
PMI has supported training, refresher training, supportive supervision, provision of job aids, and other activities to improve delivery of malaria interventions in primary health care and secondary health facilities in 11 PMI-supported states.

PMI continues to face enormous challenges in supporting capacity building. Program coordination at all levels remains difficult given overlapping partner support and gaps in some states. State and LGA-level capacity in management and technical oversight varies considerably among the PMI-supported states. Health workers reassignments occur frequently even at the national level. Commodity stockouts impede health workers' ability to implement the training they have received, and to provide critical services. Last year, a national health worker strike that lasted several months led to closure of health facilities, expiration of health commodities, and lack of reporting to state levels.

In the last 18 months, the NFELTP focused on providing experiential epidemiological training to 30 residents (5 in cohort 6, 12 in cohort 7 and 13 in cohort 8). The two-year training focuses on epidemiological investigations, outbreak investigations, and SM&E of malaria. Residents have engaged in malaria related activities including support for data analysis, research, HMIS, and surveillance. The NFELTP program deployed residents at NMEP, states, and PMI implementing partners to serve in various capacities. They supported case management units in Oyo and Ebonyi states; assisted in evaluation of surveillance systems for NMEP and Benue, Ondo, and Oyo States; supported analysis of routine and survey data for decision making for NMEP and Benue, Ondo, and Oyo States; analysis of rapid health facility assessment data for Kogi State; and, participated in cascade training on harmonized HMIS tools in Zamfara, Kogi, and Oyo States. In July 2015 a hands-on writing skills workshop was held to support residents develop their thesis into publishable manuscripts. So far, five of the manuscripts were completed and submitted for publication in peer reviewed journals. PMI is supporting NFELTP to design a malaria short course that would increase state-level epidemiological capacity to monitor and report on malaria trends.

PMI supported NSTOP to finalize the implementation work plan for the NSTOP/Malaria Frontline project in Kano and Zamfara states, and review of the malaria training materials. The project is a collaborative effort between PMI, NMEP, State governments of Kano and Zamfara,

NSTOP, and NFELTP. The NSTOP/Malaria Frontline project has recruited key personnel including a national supervisor, a national training coordinator, and two state supervisors for Kano and Zamfara states. The project has hired 34 LGA level NSTOP/Malaria officers for Kano and Zamfara. PMI assisted in the development of a malaria intervention assessment protocol to be used as the baseline survey for the NSTOP/Malaria Frontline project to allow comparability. The baseline will be done in July 2016 in Kano and Zamfara states.

Plans and justification
Given Nigeria's large population, decentralized health system, and multiple donors, the NMEP must coordinate its own activities and those of partners to ensure efficiency and high program impact. Although Nigeria is operating a decentralized health system, the NMEP has retained the functions of policy-setting; developing strategies, implementation guidelines, and training materials; standardizing training and SBCC materials; maintaining the quality of care; and training health workers. Responding to emergencies such as malaria outbreaks also remains a core responsibility of the NMEP. Given these responsibilities, in addition to coordinating all malaria control activities in the country, NMEP is a critical organization and strengthening their technical and management capacity is important.

At the same time, the states and LGAs are the operational levels of the malaria elimination program in Nigeria where implementation and service delivery happen. The most important program outcomes occur at the state level, making strengthening of state and LGA-level management and technical capacity absolutely essential to any programmatic success. Consequently, PMI will continue such support at all three levels—national, state, and LGA—to effectively and efficiently plan, implement, coordinate, monitor, and evaluate malaria control program interventions. PMI investment will include supporting the national level to develop policy and strategic documents, revising training and SBCC guidelines, developing standard operating procedures, conducting monitoring visits, supporting coordination meetings, and training.

At the state level, PMI will support malaria coordination at state and LGA level, training of health workers, supportive supervision, and review meetings for data use. A key component of this work will be using the routine DHIS2 data that are collected in states to guide programmatic decision-making in addition to indicator reporting. Capitalizing on this opportunity will play a major role in PMI's ability to improve service provision in its focus states.

FY 2017 funds will be used to support NMEP and state malaria managers to attend key malaria scientific conferences, such as the American Society of Tropical Medicine and Hygiene Annual Conference in the USA, the malaria M&E course in Ghana, and Roll Back Malaria Regional Meetings.

PMI will continue to support NFELTP to train residents in malaria epidemiology. This will include didactic lectures as well as support for fieldwork and malaria research as prioritized by NMEP and PMI. The program will organize a malaria scientific meeting to disseminate the epidemiological findings of residents. The program will also support data management activities including training at state and LGA levels, including data retrieval, analysis, and data quality assessments. The FY 2017 funds will also support: publication of findings from malaria related research; NMEP-NFELTP joint scientific workshop and new project proposal development; training residents on DHIS2; and participation in developing NMEP guidelines for OR. NFELTP will implement a malaria short course for state-level epidemiologists whose objective is to increase state-level epidemiological capacity to monitor and report on malaria trends that can inform state-level program planning.

Table 13: Health Systems Strengthening Activities

HSS Building Block	Technical Area	Description of Activity
Health Services	Case Management	<ul><li>Expand training/refresher training of health workers in malaria case management to more health facilities in each state.</li><li>Strengthen the capacity for QA and quality control for malaria diagnostic services through training and supervision.</li><li>Strengthen malaria policy through support for Drug Therapeutic Efficacy Testing studies in five sites.</li><li>Expand the training and service quality for malaria diagnosis in the private sector.</li></ul>
	Prevention of MIP	<ul><li>Training of health workers in prevention of MIP and new IPTp policy.</li><li>Scale up the implementation of IPTp.</li><li>Strengthening the capacity for delivery of IPTp DOT and proper recording of IPTp and ITNs in HMIS register.</li><li>Develop capacity for using data to monitor IPTp coverage and dropout rates for IPTp2 and IPTp3.</li></ul>
Health Workforce	Health Systems Strengthening	<ul><li>Build, through training and technical assistance, host country managerial and leadership capacity for effective malaria control.</li><li>Support training of NMEP and SMEP staff on M&E, data analysis, reporting, and use.</li><li>Support for training of epidemiologists under the NFELTP program.</li></ul>
Health Information	M&E	<ul><li>Strengthen disease surveillance systems to improve decision-making, planning, forecasting and program management.</li><li>Develop capacities for data analysis and use of data for decision making.</li></ul>
	Operational	<ul><li>Develop capacities for identifying operational research</li></ul>

HSS Building Block	Technical Area	Description of Activity
	Research	questions, writing concept papers, developing protocols, and writing manuscripts.
Essential Medical Products, Vaccines, and Technologies	Case Management, MIP, and ITNs	• Strengthen NMEP and state capacities for forecasting and quantification, procurement planning, and storage of malaria commodities. • Provide technical assistance for developing LMCUs and use of LMIS for management of stocks. • Reinforce capacities for stores management, including record keeping. • Develop the capacity for management of electronic data base at state ware house and electronic LMIS.
Health Finance	Health Systems Strengthening	• Provide technical assistance to leverage financial contributions and services from private sector partners (i.e. extractive industries) for malaria prevention and control. • Support NMEP and states to participate in national and regional forums with private sector and work with private sector health alliances.
Leadership and Governance	Health Systems Strengthening	• Strengthen national coordinating and regulatory bodies to direct and manage malaria resources, develop guidelines, and improve quality of services. • Strengthen the regulatory function of the national drug authorities through support for monitoring ACTs and regional laboratories. • Advocacy meetings with state leadership armed with targets and funding needs for action plans to mobilize resources.

Proposed activities with FY 2017 funding ($2,000,000):

1. *Support the NMEP to strengthen technical capacity at national level:* FY 2017 funds will be used to support NMEP's role as the lead coordination body through meeting support, monitoring support, and training. FY 2017 funds will be used to support NMEP to attend key malaria scientific conferences, Roll Back Malaria Regional Meetings, and meetings to revise and develop policies, strategic documents, guidelines, and training materials as well as technical assistance to states, and other related activities. *($500,000)*

2. *Support for capacity building to the states and LGAs.* PMI will strengthen the capacity for planning, management, and delivery of malaria interventions at state, LGA, and health facility levels. The capacity building under HSS is targeting the top-level and

midlevel managers at the state, LGA, and the in-charges of health facilities, as well as the professional and regulatory bodies. The capacity building interventions will include pre-service training, supportive supervision, and SM&E capacity of state and LGA health workers. The capacity building activities will be extended to the medical, laboratory, pharmaceutical, nursing/midwifery, and PPMV professional regulatory bodies and associations, and will include providing MIP and case management guidelines and SOPs. *($1,000,000)*

3. *Support for the NFELTP:* Support training for ten NMEP and SMEP personnel for the two-year NFELTP course, including the malaria short course. The cost of training per trainee $50,000/year. The course will target state epidemiologists to further their capacity for surveillance, monitoring, and evaluation related to malaria. *($500,000)*

5. Social and behavior change communication

NMEP/PMI objectives
Social and behavior change communication (SBCC) is a core component of the NMSP 2014-2020 and outlines the NMEP's priorities for this period. At the NMEP, the SBCC strategy is managed by the ACSM subcommittee which consists of Roll Back Malaria partners, including PMI and the ACSM branch of the NMEP. The ACSM branch serves as the secretariat for the ACSM subcommittee. The ACSM subcommittee assists the NMEP to coordinate and provide technical oversight to SBCC activities in malaria.

The ACSM strategy aims to maintain high coverage of malaria prevention and treatment practices, increase demand for these services, improve use and delivery of malaria control interventions, enhance political will and an enabling environment for malaria control activities, and improve ACSM coordination at national, state, and local government levels.

The NMEP ACSM objective and target is to provide adequate information to all Nigerians such that at least 80% of the populace habitually takes appropriate malaria preventive and treatment measures as necessary by 2020.

Strategies:
1. Maintain high knowledge of malaria prevention and treatment practices.
2. Improve demand for, and use of malaria prevention and management services.
3. Enhance political will and enabling environment for malaria control/elimination activities.
4. Scale up facilities-based dissemination of appropriate information for malaria prevention and management practices.
5. Improve ACSM coordination at all levels.

Targets:

1. To reach 100% of Nigerians aged five years and above with sustained information, education, and communication about prevention and management of malaria by 2020.
2. To advocate to at least 80% of targeted political leaders, policy-makers and the private sector leaders for adequate, timely, and sustained funding of malaria control activities by 2020.
3. To ensure that at least 80% of individuals visiting health facilities receive information for malaria prevention and management by 2020.
4. To ensure that at least 80% of individuals visiting health facilities receive information at the community level (schools, community and faith-based organizations, etc.) on malaria prevention and management by 2020.
5. To set up functional ACSM core groups in all the states and the Federal Capital Territory by 2016.
6. To ensure that 80% of pregnant women and children under five years of age use ITNs by 2018.

Progress since PMI was launched
Since its inception in 2011, PMI/Nigeria has supported a variety of SBCC activities aimed at supporting demand and uptake of key interventions and strengthening the capacity of the ACSM branch of the NMEP.

In 2014, the PMI SBCC program was reviewed to strategically focus on segmented target audiences, channels, and specific behavioral goals. The program developed a results framework that provided a defined strategy for monitoring and tracking of implementation and outcomes. PMI consolidated all SBCC interventions into one mechanism. This approach provided cross-cutting SBCC interventions to complement malaria prevention and case management interventions.

In the 11 PMI-supported states, SBCC activities were implemented through various channels: mass media, community groups, and interpersonal activities to specifically motivate positive behaviors relevant for malaria control. This has largely focused on ITN use and care, improving ANC attendance, and instilling prompt case management-seeking behavior. PMI broadly employed mass media communications through television and radio that promoted awareness of malaria issues. This is reinforced at community level with IPC through volunteers at the community level to motivate, raise awareness, and encourage positive care seeking and prevention behaviors. PMI's community intervention strategy used different community structures to facilitate IPC sessions through household visits and community dialogues.

The SBCC program explored the use of other relevant channels to disseminate malaria messages in order to increase coverage of messages. For instance, IPC was employed to influence health worker behaviors and compliance with test results as well as increasing the frequency and quality of information provided by facility-based and community health workers to clients. PMI funding also supported journalists to identify and develop appropriate malaria news items, and trained leaders of various faith-based denominations as IPC agents for their congregation.

PMI provided support to update the ACSM guide to reflect current SBCC priorities, and to guide states in planning and implementing SBCC programs in line with the NMSP 2014-2020. The guide provides an integrated communication plan that standardizes messages and tools for all partners, with the understanding that states may need to adapt it to their specific demographic and cultural situations. The PMI-supported states developed an ACSM guide that can be used to engage in strategic-level advocacy and resource mobilization for malaria control with PMI assistance. PMI funds were used to develop the SBCC capacities of state and national program staff through short-term training and technical assistance.

According to the preliminary 2015 NMIS, 36% of women surveyed had heard a message about malaria in the previous six weeks to the survey. Three common sources of messages were radio (70%), television (32%) and community workers (17%). However, only three percent of respondents heard malaria messages from a church or mosque. Seeing or hearing a message on malaria was associated with education level and higher wealth quintiles.

Progress during the past 12-18 months

Malaria-free Campaign
PMI FY2015 funds were used to continue support of the 'malaria-free' campaign that was launched in 2014. The objective of the campaign is to increase awareness of the burden of malaria by raising the perception of risk of malaria infection among the population. The campaign was designed to respond the results of the 2010 NMIS survey which showed that low perception of malaria risk and poor practices related to malaria are common in Nigeria. The mass media campaign creates general awareness of malaria, and reinforces key behavior change messages. Messages aired through mass media channels (radio and television) were reinforced through IPC channels at the community or household level. The national campaign consisted of a malaria song/anthem called 'Play Your Part' that emphasized the need for every Nigerian to play their part in malaria control by: sleeping inside a mosquito net every night; promptly testing all fevers with RDTs; taking an ACT if a malaria test is positive; and urging women to attend ANC centers during pregnancy. The popularity of the song was reinforced by regular airing on two national- and state-level radio stations. About 8.5 million people were reached through this campaign across the 11 PMI-supported states.

PMI, in collaboration with other development partners such as the Bill and Melinda Gates Foundation, funded an educational-entertainment TV series called 'Newman Street.' This television serial drama uses family-oriented characters to educate on the various aspects of malaria prevention and control while motivating behavior change by appealing to the emotions of audiences that might find in common between themselves and the characters in the drama series. The first season of the 'Newman Street' drama was broadcast on two national-level television stations and 13 state-level television stations. 'Play Your Part' and 'Newman Street' are also available through online and social media platforms to broadcast to the rapidly growing information technology-savvy populations at national level. Global Fund investments in SBCC rely heavily on community mobilization as a channel to increase ITN use during the post-campaign period. In the nine states where Global Fund overlaps with PMI investment, the community level activities occur in separate LGAs and communities. This strategy allows more communities to be reached with SBCC activities, thereby increasing the scale and coverage of community mobilization. The NMEP partners including PMI, through the ACSM subcommittee, ensure that all SBCC investments are coordinated to avoid duplication of efforts in states where activities overlap. This is done by ensuring that all NMEP partners produce maps of partner-level SBCC activities, and then the NMEP develops a national map of all activities with state and LGA level details. This process is done annually by the ACSM sub-committee.

Community outreach and engagement through action learning platforms
Activities focused on intensifying community-level interventions for malaria prevention, case management, and prevention of MIP. PMI supported community mobilization activities, including community dialogue, compound meetings, and house-to-house visits by trained community volunteers. Emphasis was placed on community-focused sessions (rather than on individual sessions) to increase coverage. These volunteers used flip-cards to keep messaging consistent and provide visual aids to reinforce messages. Over 235,000 households were visited in PMI-supported states. In total, 940,000 people out of a population of an estimated 52 million people in PMI-supported states were reached through IPC with messages on ITN ownership and use, prompt care-seeking for fever, severe malaria, and on prevention and management of MIP. Over 16,000 pregnant women were referred to attend ANC through the community mobilization efforts. PMI also supported sensitization of religious and traditional leaders to mainstream malaria messages in sermons and public speeches. Over 5,000 opinion leaders were reached.

Capacity building for national and state malaria programs
In PMI focus states, the state malaria focal persons are supported by state-level ACSM technical committees, which were established with PMI support. In general, all PMI supported states have adopted and adapted the national ACSM guide as a basis for state-level operations. PMI continues to support quarterly meetings of the state-level ACSM committees and Ward Development Committees to improve the quality of SBCC activities in communities
PMI has also supported the ACSM branch to develop an annual advocacy plan that provides more methodology and structure to advocacy activities in the country.

ITN campaign support
PMI implemented specific SBCC activities to improve ITN uptake, use and care behaviors in four PMI-supported states that implemented ITN mass campaigns in the past year. State-wide mass media messages were aired through radio channels; communities were mobilized by using Town Announcers (individuals whose role in the community was to relay messages to the people), traditional and religious leaders. SBCC activities continued for a period of six weeks post-campaign through house-to-house visits in communities identified as having low hanging rates from the post campaign end-process evaluation.

Monitoring

In 2015, PMI fielded formative research in three PMI-supported states (Akwa Ibom, Kebbi, and Nasarawa); each state is in a different geographical zone to allow for a more generalizable result. The results showed that knowledge for malaria and interventions was relatively high across the different zones however, misconceptions were very common. For instance, a significant number of respondents believed that prolonged exposure to sunlight could cause malaria infection. Social norms were strong determinants of positive behaviors. For instance, households are motivated to sleep inside the ITNs if they think their neighbors were doing the same. PMI/Nigeria is using the DHIS2 platform to monitor SBCC outcomes indicators like IPTp coverage, malaria test rates, and ACT use. PMI/Nigeria is collaborating with the White House / Social Behavioral Science Team to evaluate the use of community health workers to improve ANC attendance and IPTp coverage in Kebbi State. This will provide valuable information on the effectiveness of focused SBCC interventions in improving ANC attendance and uptake of IPTp at the health facilities. PMI/Nigeria will also conduct secondary analysis of the 2015 MIS to evaluate the performance of SBCC interventions. This analysis will aim to identify most effective channels of communication, barriers to desired behaviors and effectiveness of interventions by comparing intervention states to states without SBCC interventions.

Proposed activities with FY 2017 funding ($5,000,000)
SBCC efforts will continue to focus on increasing net use, IPTp, testing for malaria before treatment, compliance to test results, and correct care-seeking behavior. SBCC messages will continue to be delivered through various channels although PMI will better direct interventions based on evidence from the 2015 NMIS and the routine HMIS data, which will help to identify LGAs and health facilities catchment areas that are under-performing in malaria control activities. These areas will then benefit from more intensive SBCC activities. Rural and poor communities will be prioritized so as to address equity gaps reflected in 2015 NMIS.

Mass media

1. *Integrated 'malaria-free' campaign in PMI supported state:* PMI will continue to support integrated advocacy and social mobilization for national malaria communication activities. These activities sustain the 'malaria–free campaign' and utilize the national malaria song, educational radio, and television drama shows. The national-level mass media will be targeted to reach at least 20% of all households, i.e. approximately 35 million Nigerians, in one year. The messages will be integrated along the technical areas in the malaria program. Again, leveraging the standardized messages from the national 'malaria-free' campaign, PMI will tailor mass media approaches to the relevant audiences in the 11 PMI-supported states. Mass media activities will aim to increase use of treated nets, promote appropriate malaria case management, and improve ANC attendance and increase IPTp uptake. Depending on demographic, socioeconomic, and epidemiological profiles, PMI will develop SBCC activities that use mass media to effectively reach target populations and support services provided by through case management and prevention interventions. This will reach approximately 56 million people. *($1,200,000)*

Community mobilization and interpersonal communication

2. *Community outreach and engagement:* Community leadership structures and potential champions such as religious and community leaders, civil society organizations, and opinion leaders will be engaged through group dialogues to mobilize behavior change in communities. Household and community interactive sessions using IPC will be carried out in communities in the 11 PMI-supported states. This will reach about 5 million people and focus on delivering messages to promote net usage and preventative care, ANC attendance, and the risks of MIP and correct care-seeking behavior. HIMS facility data will be used to determine communities that would be prioritized in these outreach activities. *(1,500,000)*

3. *SMC:* Focused community mobilization and communication activities will be done to promote sustained adherence to SMC throughout the campaign period. ($300,000)

Service provider initiatives

Health workers are a key target of IPC activities. Even with training and supervision, poor practices, particularly around malaria diagnosis, are still observed. These are often driven by misguided perceptions of the utility of diagnostic tools. To address this, PMI will work to use respected medical and academic figures to address these issues and improve practices around case management and IPTp delivery.

4. *RDT use and trust*: This activity will be carried out in the 11 PMI-supported states with the aim to improve service providers' testing of fevers by RDTs and compliance with test results. Service provider engagements and group interactive sessions will aim to improve provider-patient interactions and compliance of service providers with RDT results. *($700,000)*

5. *IPTp uptake:* In the 11 PMI-supported states, IPC activities will be carried out with ANC health workers to promote IPTp 1, 2, and 3+ uptake. This will leverage the training to health workers on MIP. During community mobilization activities and routine ANC outreach, traditional birth attendants and private midwives will be encouraged to refer clients for IPTp in health facilities. The SBCC activities will be integrated into the outreach IPTp campaigns in selected states in Nigeria. *($400,000)*

Promoting appropriate use of ITNs

6. *ITN campaign:* SBCC activities will support the demand creation and communication aspects of ITN mass distribution campaigns. Activities will include use of mass media, town announcers, and advocacy through religious and traditional leaders. Intensive post-campaign activities will continue up until six weeks after the distribution campaign through house-to-house mobilization to reinforce net use and care actions. *($600,000)*

7. *School-based SBCC campaign*: PMI will conduct school-based campaigns to engage primary school students in PMI-supported states in order to generate discussions around positive behaviors necessary for malaria prevention, diagnosis, and treatment. This will rely on the

theory that young children can drive positive behavior change within households in Nigeria. *($300,000)*

8. Monitoring: More emphases will be put into measuring program outcomes in focus states. The PMI program will explore ways to understand the influence of specific interventions on performance of key behavior indicators in supported states. With FY 2016 funds, PMI plans to do a secondary analysis of the 2015 MIS and other relevant survey data to determine the effectiveness of the various channels of communication, and generate lessons learned to inform future SBCC activities.

6. Surveillance, monitoring, and evaluation

NMEP/PMI objectives

Surveillance, monitoring, and evaluation (SM&E) is an integral part of the NMSP 2014-2020, with one of the primary objectives focusing on routine collection and reporting of malaria data, and use of such data for program improvement. In 2009, the NMEP developed the National M&E Plan for Malaria Control in Nigeria. The M&E plan was reviewed in 2014 to align with the NMSP 2014-2020. The NMEP SM&E TWG led the process for developing the M&E plan, with support and participation from a broad group of partners including the PMI, Global Fund, WHO, World Bank, UNICEF, DfID, and local NGOs.

The NMEP M&E plan covers three main areas: 1) strengthening routine malaria information systems; 2) supporting periodic household surveys; and 3) improving OR to ensure that new intervention strategies are evidence-based. The primary objective of the M&E Plan for Malaria Control in Nigeria is to establish a sound and continuously updated database that monitors progress towards agreed targets, evaluates outcomes and impact, and is used to effectively manage and adjust interventions based on evidence. Strategies of the M&E plan include:

- Improve collection, quality and utilization of routine data to monitor the implementation of malaria related interventions to feed into the HMIS.
- Periodically evaluate the progress of malaria control with respect to outcome and impact indicators through appropriate data collection processes.
- Strengthen links between the research community and NMEP, and its development and implementation partners in order to ensure that ongoing research is oriented towards the key operational questions and can provide the necessary evidence to continuously improve interventions for malaria control.
- Provide a road map for coordination of malaria–related SM&E among partners.

Progress since PMI was launched

The PMI SM&E approach in Nigeria contributes to the NMEP M&E plan 2014-2020. Specifically, PMI supports strengthening the routine HMIS at various levels of the health system; periodic population-based surveys such as the Nigeria Malaria Indicator Survey (2015 NMIS), the Nigeria Demographic and Health Survey (2013 NDHS), and the 2015 facility-based malaria implementation assessment (MIA) that are used to measure the status of key malaria indicators; and OR to guide programmatic decisions (see Table 14).

Table 14: Malaria Data Sources, Nigeria, 2010-2017

Data source	Survey activities	Year									
		2009	2010	2011	2012	2013	2014	2015	2016	2017	2018
Household surveys	Demographic and Health Survey (DHS)**					X					X
	Malaria Indicator Survey (MIS)		X					X			
	ACT Watch Surveys (Household)*	X			X						
	SMART Survey*					X		X		(X)	
	Multiple Indicator Cluster Survey (MICS)*			X					X		
	Media Impact Surveys*						X				
	Omnibus Surveys**	X	X	X	X	X	X	X	X	(X)	(X)
	National AIDS and Reproductive Health Survey (NARHS)*					X					
Health facility and other surveys	ACT Watch Surveys (Outlet)*	X			X	X					
	Rapid Impact Assessment (RIA)*					X	X				
	Malaria Implementation Assessment (MIA)								X		
	End-use verification (EUV)	X	X	X	X	X	X	X	X	(X)	(X)

	Service Delivery Index (SDI)*						X				
Malaria surveillance and routine system support***	NMEP malaria parasite sentinel surveillance (MPSS) system*								(X)	(X)	(X)
	Support to HMIS**	X	X	X	X	X	X	X	X	(X)	(X)
Therapeutic efficacy monitoring	*In vivo* efficacy monitoring	X				X			X		(X)
Entomology	Entomological surveillance and resistance monitoring				X	X	X	X	X	(X)	(X)
Net durability monitoring	ITN monitoring								X	(X)	(X)

Notes:

- Surveys with an asterisk (*) are not funded by PMI but some may receive other U.S. Government funding. The MICS and SMART receive USAID funding.
- Surveys with double asterisks (**) are partially funded with PMI funds.
- The MPSS is to happen in 2016, 2017 and 2018. The HMIS is for all facilities, while the MPSS will be for sentinel health facilities to provide real time quality data on malaria testing, positivity rates, and ACT use.

Routine Health Information System

In 2012, Nigeria adopted a harmonized approach to collecting routine malaria data through the national HMIS that is managed by the FMoH Department of Planning, Research and Statistics. HMIS data are reported monthly from public health facilities to the LGA level using standardized facility-level aggregate data tools (paper based). The LGA HMIS focal persons (health information officers) collate and enter malaria data received by health facilities into the DHIS2 application. Health facility level aggregated data are then immediately available for review and analysis by state and national malaria elimination officials. Data quality reviews from state and national levels can prompt LGA verification and if necessary, data correction is done within two months of data entry. LGA health information officers are currently the sole control points for data entry or correction for any health facility within their LGAs. State and national health information officers are unable to enter or modify data in the DHIS2 system.

The NMEP and malaria partners participated in the process that produced the standardized HMIS tools for data collection and entry into the DHIS2 application. With partner support, Nigeria started to implement the harmonized HMIS tools in 2013. PMI assisted in developing the instructional manual and the trainer's guide, and supported the national training of trainers in Abuja. Nationwide training was completed in 2014. DHIS2 has since been the sole routine information system used for malaria data in Nigeria. Although Nigeria has an Integrated Disease

Surveillance and Response System to report weekly disease counts for epidemic prone diseases, current case definitions for malaria do not align with the NMEP supported definition. Therefore this system is not used for malaria reporting. PMI supported the training of 10,668 of 43,321 (25%) health workers in SM&E.

National Surveys

In 2010, an NMEP-sponsored NMIS was completed and provided pre-PMI baseline estimates for most of the coverage indicators used by PMI. In 2013 PMI supported a NDHS which included a malaria module; however, the NDHS did not collect biomarkers.

Health Facility and Other Surveys

PMI has been supporting EUV surveys from 2012 through 2015. The EUV surveys are done every six months to assess stock availability of malaria commodities in health facilities and warehouses, testing for malaria before treatment, prescription of ACTs for uncomplicated malaria, storage conditions for malaria commodities, and training of health workers in the various areas they work. Bi-annual reports are provided summarizing the EUV activities and findings. These reports provide key observations, recommendations, and next steps for commodity distribution. However, EUV survey results are not statistically representative.

Program Monitoring

Since 2011, PMI has supported the Mission-wide M&E services contract which oversees a broad range of M&E services such as: performance monitoring (via a web-based reporting system); M&E capacity building for Mission staff and implementing partners; data quality assessment (DQA) for indicators, and performance evaluation of activities. The web-based performance monitoring system collects and stores activity-level indicators, including all required annual PMI output indicators. Implementing partners enter performance data quarterly and upload their narrative reports that serve as data sources.

Progress during the past 12-18 months

PMI is the co-chair of the M&E technical sub-committee of NMEP which: (1) coordinates efforts for strengthening the HMIS, (2) oversees the planning and implementation of various surveys and assessments, and (3) coordinates SM&E activities with other partners.

In the past year, PMI has continued the support for HMIS strengthening at national and state levels. This support includes capacity building of health workers at all levels, periodic DQA, and the roll-out of the DHIS2. PMI also supported the coordination of SM&E efforts, including LGA data collection, consolidation and QA meetings to improve completeness and timeliness of HMIS data in PMI-supported states. Furthermore, PMI supported state and federal data consultative meetings as well as the NMEP M&E sub-committee meetings to facilitate standardized malaria data collection across the geo-political zones. PMI uses data generated by DHIS2 for the bi-annual Mission portfolio review, PMI Annual Report to Congress, and the Malaria and Mission Operational Plans.

Routine Health Information System
One objective of the NMSP 2014-2020 is for 80% of health facilities in all LGAs to report routinely on malaria by 2020, that progress is measured, and that the evidence is used for program improvement. In 2013, only 40% of health facilities submitted their monthly reports, and only 47% of health facilities submitted their reports in a timely manner. The latest national reporting rate for 2015 is over 60% but ranges from 50% to 95% in individual states. Since 2013, the 11 PMI-supported states have performed better than the non-PMI states, and better than the national reporting rate (see figure 8).

Figure 8: Annual Reporting Rates for PMI and Non-PMI focus states

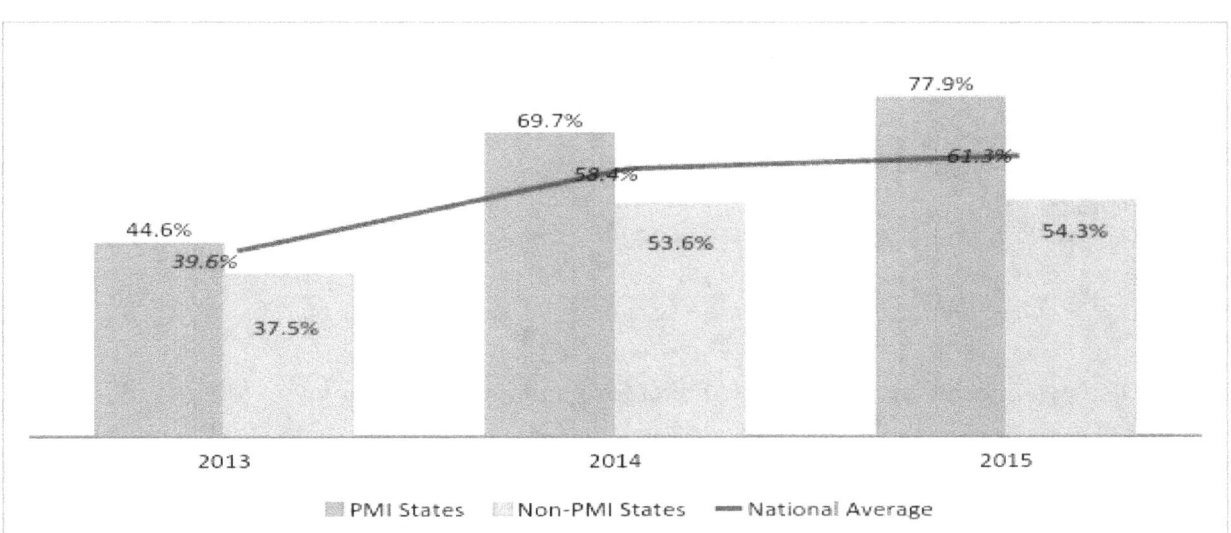

With increased DHIS2 implementation, PMI has supported training of health workers and provided feedback to data collectors. PMI also supported DQA and routine LGA data validation meetings in nine states. As a result, completeness and timeliness have significantly improved in the PMI-supported states, as illustrated in figure 9.

Figure 9: DHIS2 reporting rates National and PMI focus states

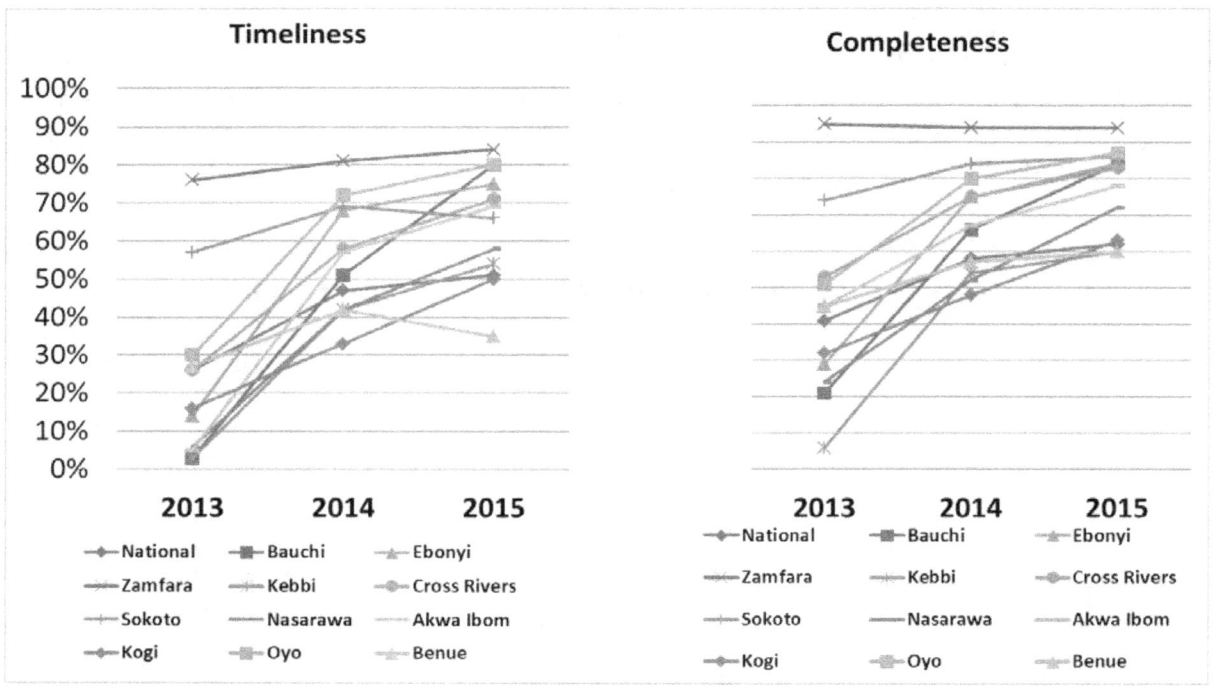

There is also evidence of increasing use of data for planning the procurement of commodities and other resources. All the 11 PMI-supported states have developed Annual Operational Plans for malaria based on some of the data from the HMIS. Timely and complete data reporting on malaria from the health facility to the LGAs, and subsequently to the state and national levels, has improved in PMI-supported states. However, more work is needed to improve data quality and supportive supervision. Inadequate reporting at the facility level is the result of several factors: insufficient training in data capture, compilation, and storage, lack of motivation, inadequate supportive supervision, and little accountability or feedback. Historically NMEP's ability to make timely programmatic decisions using HMIS has been problematic; however, the use of DHIS2 provides an opportunity to greatly improve the access, availability, and timeliness of consistent malaria information for programmatic decision making. PMI supports SM&E personnel in the 11 PMI-supported states, who facilitate the HMIS harmonization process and national efforts to strengthen the information system. Table 15 shows SM&E indicators available in DHIS2 for the period of January – December 2015.

Table 15: Routine Surveillance Indicators, 2015

INDICATORS	VALUE	COMMENTS
1. **Total number of reported malaria cases** Data source: HMIS/DHIS2	14,732,359	
Total diagnostically confirmed cases	8,217,802	< 5yrs: 3,471,546 ≥ 5 yrs: 4,746,256
Total clinical/presumed/unconfirmed cases	6,525,557	< 5yrs: 2,999,163 ≥ 5 yrs: 3,526,394
If available, report separately for outpatients and inpatients		
Outpatient number of reported malaria cases		Not reported in HMIS
Inpatient number of reported malaria cases		Not reported in HMIS
2. **Total number of reported malaria deaths**		Not reported in HMIS
3. **Malaria test positivity rate (outpatients)** Data source: HMIS/DHIS2	71.6%	Data includes both microscopy **and** RDT
Numerator: Number of outpatient confirmed malaria cases	8,127,073	
Denominator: Number of outpatients receiving a diagnostic test for malaria (RDT or microscopy)	11,355,426	
4. **Completeness of monthly health facility reporting** Data source: HMIS/DHIS2	61.9%	
Numerator: Number of monthly reports received from health facilities	249,161	
Denominator: Number of health facility reports expected (i.e., number of facilities expected to report multiplied by the number of months considered	402,552	

The FMoH planned an assessment of HMIS in 2015 but it did not take place. In the interim, PMI is conducting a MIA to examine the outcome of HMIS investments in four PMI-supported states.

Household Surveys
With funding from PMI, Global Fund, DfID, and UNICEF, the NMEP, in partnership with the National Population Council and the National Bureau of Statistics, implemented the 2015 NMIS

from October 2015 through November 2015. PMI provided funding for technical assistance, procurement of supplies, data collection and analysis, production of the preliminary and final reports, and dissemination of the results. The preliminary results were made available in March 2016, and the final analyses are expected in September 2016. Although results are still preliminary and are not analyzed at the state level, the country as a whole did see a marked 36% decrease in malaria prevalence measured by microscopy in children age 6-59 months (42% in 2010; 27% in 2015). By zones, malaria prevalence varied from 37% in the North West Zone to 14% in the South East Zone.

Health Facility Surveys and Assessments
With FY 2015 funds, PMI is supporting the MIA during 2016. The goal of the MIA is to document progress in malaria control interventions between 2008 and 2014 in Cross River, Ebonyi, Nasarawa, and Sokoto States. The specific objectives of the MIA are: (1) to describe state-level malaria interventions in the four states; (2) to document changes in key malaria case management indicators; (3) to assess quality of care among the PMI-supported and non-PMI-supported primary health care facilities; (4) to assess the quality of monthly malaria data for select indicators at health facilities; (5) to assess trends in malaria morbidity and mortality at the hospital level following the scale-up of malaria control interventions in Nasarawa (2008-2013) and Sokoto (2005-2013) states; and (6) to document changes in the contextual factors likely to affect malaria interventions and outcomes.

Overall, the results of the MIA will provide NMEP and PMI with a greater understanding of what has been achieved in the four states in regard to the state-level coverage of malaria interventions and the facility-level quality of malaria case management. The results will also show what has worked best, and what still needs to be improved. In addition, it will provide information about the quality of the facility data in the DHIS2 system, and show what needs to be strengthened. Finally, the MIA will allow NMEP and PMI to draw lessons learned from the documented experiences in the four states, and strengthen the design and implementation of future interventions.

Data collection for this assessment ended in June. The data analysis is ongoing, and preliminary results are expected in August 2016. The findings from the assessment, along with other relevant malaria SM&E data, will be used to inform programmatic decisions, identify gaps, and provide information for future program planning. The findings will also be used to revise and update HMIS tools.

National Nutrition and Health Survey (NNHS)
The NNHS is an annual household survey implemented by the Nigerian National Bureau of Statistics (NBS), with technical assistance from UNICEF and financial support from USAID and other development partners. NNHS is conducted using Standardized Monitoring and Assessment of Relief and Transition (SMART) methods. The 2015 edition was the second national level survey thus far. The NNHS provides up-to-date information on the status of nutrition and health including malaria, and measures key indicators that support the country in monitoring progress towards national goals. Malaria indicators measured by this survey include ITN coverage and

use, malaria testing of fever cases, treatment with ACTs, and provision of SP to pregnant women.

Multiple Indicator Cluster Survey (MICS)
The Nigeria MICS was carried out by the NBS. Financial and technical support was provided by UNICEF, the United Nations Population Fund, and the Government of Nigeria. MICS is a household survey developed by UNICEF, which provides up-to-date information on the situation of children and women, and measures key indicators that allows countries to monitor progress towards the Millennium Development Goals and the Sustainable Development Goals. Currently, the fifth round of MICS is ongoing, and preliminary findings will be available in early 2017. Malaria indicators measured by this survey include ITN coverage and use, testing of fever cases for malaria, treatment with ACT, and provision of SP for pregnant women.

Media Impact Survey
The Media Impact Survey provides information on community members such as knowledge, attitudes and practices in relation to malaria transmission and control before the roll-out of SBCC interventions. The Global Fund supported the first survey in 2014 to assess the previous investments in SBCC.

Nigerian Omnibus Survey *(Nigerbus)*
The *Nigerbus* survey is a market research study conducted semiannually by research organizations to collect data for various subscribing organizations. The survey affords companies and development partners in Nigeria a cost-effective opportunity to ask questions relevant to their activities, without the extra burden of organizing a full-fledged stand-alone survey. PMI buys into *Nigerbus* to provide information about SBCC, specifically to answer questions on knowledge, attitudes and practices related to malaria core interventions.

Plans and justification
PMI/Nigeria's surveillance, monitoring, and evaluating activities will continue to rely on a combination of routine malaria data collected through the HMIS and the LMIS, household surveys, health facility surveys and assessments, and information from partners.

With FY 2017 funds, PMI will continue to strengthen the routine malaria information system at the health facility, LGA, state, and national levels through the harmonized HMIS (using the DHIS2). The objective is to achieve at least 80% on-time reporting of malaria cases by LGAs and 80% by functioning health facilities in PMI-supported states by 2020. PMI will support the revision and finalization of the malaria information system data collection tools, as part of the overall USG support to strengthen the Nigeria HMIS. PMI will also support training, refresher training, and supportive supervision in HMIS in PMI-supported states with special emphasis on malaria.

The supportive supervisions will improve proper documentation and reporting of malaria and other diseases in a timely manner using national standardized tools. Strengthening LGA capacity is a priority as the SM&E officers at this level are the only people able to enter or modify data in the DHIS2. PMI will support state SM&E officials to perform supportive supervision and data quality checks with LGA officers to improve proper entry into DHIS2.

Additionally, PMI will support meetings and health facility visits for larger data quality reviews and to improve use of the data at all levels. Feedback from the LGA level to specific PHCs can help to educate facilities on the seasonality of malaria cases, variations of commodity needs based on the time of year or increase in caseload, as well as to know that the data they are collecting has a higher purpose. Good quality data can be trusted and used by national, state, and LGA level SM&E officers, as well as health facility managers to help further programmatic decisions.

At the national level, PMI support of the HMIS can ensure that malaria data continues to be emphasized in the development of future data collection tools, that these tools are available at all levels, and that malaria is a focus of analysis and dashboard development using DHIS2. Continued investment in HMIS has a direct benefit to PMI and USAID/Nigeria.

PMI will consider doing further research on the reasons for non-compliance in recording accurate and timely data on the DHIS2. As this issue is not isolated to Nigeria, PMI/Nigeria will work with PMI SM&E headquarters to request support for a multi-country core-funded operational research effort to answer questions on non-compliance.

The next Nigeria DHS is scheduled for 2018, ten years after the 2008 NDHS. The 2018 NDHS will provide an opportunity for PMI to collect additional data on outcome indicators that will be used to measure progress in malaria control activities. Given the increasing availability of malaria data in Nigeria, PMI will support an effort to conduct additional analysis of available data from household surveys and routine data systems. Triangulating various data sources will further the understanding of data gaps, data quality, and provide a platform for directing resources to improve the quality and timeliness of malaria data.

PMI contributes to the Program Design and Learning (PD&L) budget for USAID/Nigeria. The PD&L budget is managed by the Nigeria USAID Mission. These funds cover external mid-term and end-line evaluation of PMI-supported programs. In FY 2016, PMI will support the evaluation of U.S. Government contributions to HMIS, and an end-line evaluation of a PMI-funded activity. The PD&L funds also contribute to the Mission-wide M&E services contract that support PMI implementing partners to: develop performance management plans; update activity performance data on the web-based reporting system; train Mission staff or implementing partner staff on relevant M&E topics; and conduct data quality assessments of PMI indicators.

Proposed activities with FY 2017 funding ($2,640,025)

1) *Strengthen routine M&E systems at national level:* Strengthen coordination and harmonization of HMIS at the FMoH and NMEP. The support includes strengthening HMIS

coordination structures, revision of the HMIS tools, and creating fora for discussing and using HMIS and other data for programmatic decisions. *($300,000)*

2) *Strengthen routine M&E systems at state level*: Strengthen the HMIS at health facility, LGA, and state levels in 11 PMI-supported states. Implementation activities will include training and supervision of data clerical staff at selected health facilities, LGAs, and states; completion of unified data collection formats; and improving collection and reporting of routine malaria indicators. *($1,800,000 [$300,000 for Bauchi and Sokoto, $1,500,000 for nine other PMI-supported states])*

4) *Support 2018 NDHS*: support the malaria module of the 2018 NDHS. The support includes technical assistance and operational costs for the survey. *($300,000)*

5) *Mission-wide M&E services contract:* PMI contribution to mission-wide M&E services. Budget is part of USAID PD&L. *($220,025)*

6) *Technical assistance for SM&E strengthening:* Two CDC TDYs to provide technical support for SM&E. *($20,000)*

7. Operational research

NMEP/PMI objectives

The 2012 Malaria Program Review (MPR) identified a lack of OR available to inform both scientific and communications-related strategy development. The NMSP 2014-2020 incorporated the MPR recommendation to convene an OR stakeholders meeting, and proposed earmarking funding in the NMEP M&E budget for OR. The earmarked funding would demonstrate the NMEP's commitment to OR. Funding was to include support to strengthen the NMEP Operational Research Unit. There is no information on actual government contributions to malaria OR beyond NMEP staff participation in donor-funded OR activities. Funding sources for malaria OR in Nigeria include DfID, the World Bank, the Bill and Melinda Gates Foundation, and the Global Fund. PMI does not contribute directly to the NMEP OR budget. The PMI contribution to malaria OR is through its implementing partners as shown in Table 16.

Progress since PMI was launched

In 2014, with WHO support, NMEP convened a research symposium, with technical input from PMI, to identify OR priority needs. The NMEP consulted with PMI in August 2014 and identified five OR priority areas for PMI funding.

In February 2016, the NMEP SM&E Branch, which oversees OR, provided PMI with updated priorities. The following general topic areas represent all activities that are on the current NMEP OR priority list.

1) **ITN category:** Continue and expand field studies on physical integrity and durability of ITNs and refine the definition of a failed net; identify laboratory tests and other accelerated testing methodology, such as resistance to damage scores, that are strongly predictive of field durability *(covered in ITN section).*

2) **ITN category:** Determine whether strategies to promote "care and repair" of ITNs can improve the physical integrity and extend the life of nets *(covered in ITN section).*

3) **Insecticide resistance category:** Conduct field evaluations of new insecticides and other strategies to mitigate or delay the spread of insecticide resistance *(covered in Entomological Monitoring section).*

4) **Case management category:** Evaluate clinician adherence to diagnostic testing and treatment including pregnancy assessment where applicable; specifically, identify factors associated with clinicians' non-adherence to diagnostic testing, and test methods to increase provider adherence at health facility and community level *(concept note approved for funding under FY 2015 MOP).*

5) **SBCC category:** Demonstrate a dose-response relationship in which a SBCC intervention results in improvements in providing timely IPTp by health care providers at the facility level, and in beneficiaries seeking and using IPTp at ANC clinics, to enable better tailoring of SBCC interventions and to improve cost-effectiveness of SBCC interventions.

To date, PMI has supported a number of OR projects that address key questions (Table 14). PMI continues to work with the NMEP to finalize new concept notes for OR projects.

The committee approved a study on evaluating clinician adherence to diagnostic testing to provide effective case management in Nigeria. Due to administrative delays, the study is expected to start in late 2016.

Table 16: Status of PMI-supported operational research

Completed OR Studies			
Title	**Start date**	**End date**	**Budget**
Feasibility of continuous distribution of ITNs through schools in Cross River	September 2012	July 2014	$341,568
Feasibility of continuous distribution of ITNs through community-based channels in Nasarawa	December 2011	July 2014	$177,074
Effects of SBCC activities on household net care and repair behaviors	April 2013	July 2014	$62,700
ITN durability in three eco-geographical zones		July 2014	
Ongoing OR Studies			
Title		**End date**	
* Evaluating clinician adherence to diagnostic testing to provide effective case management	To be determined	To be determined	$120,000
Improved community case management of childhood illnesses by proprietary patent medicine vendors	February 2015	August 2016	$500,000
No PMI-supported OR is planned currently with FY 2017 funding.			

* The clinician adherence study is awaiting the new award.

Proposed activities with FY 2017 funding ($0)

8. Staffing and administration

Two health professionals serve as resident advisors to oversee PMI in Nigeria, one representing CDC and one representing USAID. In addition, three Foreign Service Nationals (FSNs) work as part of the PMI team. Three additional FSNs dedicate 40-50% of their level of effort to the PMI/Nigeria team to provide budgeting, M&E, and logistics support. All PMI staff members are part of a single interagency team led by the USAID Mission Director or his/her designee in country. The PMI team shares responsibility for development and implementation of PMI strategies and work plans, coordination with national authorities, managing collaborating agencies and supervising day-to-day activities. Candidates for resident advisor positions (whether initial hires or replacements) will be evaluated and/or interviewed jointly by USAID and CDC, and both agencies will be involved in hiring decisions, with the final decision made by the individual hiring agency.

The PMI interagency professional staff work together to oversee all technical and administrative aspects of PMI, including finalizing details of the project design, implementing malaria prevention and treatment activities, M&E of outcomes and impact, reporting of results, and providing guidance and direction to PMI implementing partners.

The PMI lead in country is the USAID Mission Director. The day-to-day lead for PMI is delegated to the USAID Health Office Director and thus the two PMI RAs, one from USAID and one from CDC, report to the USAID Health Office Director for day-to-day leadership, and work together as a part of a single interagency team. Technical expertise housed in Atlanta and Washington complements PMI programmatic efforts.

The two PMI RAs are physically based within the USAID health office but are expected to spend approximately half of their time with and providing technical assistance to the national and state level malaria control programs and implementing partners, including time in the field monitoring program implementation and impact.

The number of locally-hired staff and necessary qualifications to successfully support PMI activities either in Ministries or in USAID will be approved by the USAID Mission Director. Because of the need to adhere to specific country policies and USAID accounting regulations, any transfer of PMI funds directly to Ministries or host governments will need to be approved by the USAID Mission Director and Controller, in addition to the U.S. Global Malaria Coordinator.

Proposed activities with FY 2017 funding: ($3,538,975)

1. *USAID in-country staff and administrative costs:* FY 2017 funds will be used to provide oversight to PMI malaria activities and technical assistance to the NMEP, and Mission-wide Administration & Oversight (A&O). Allocations for O&A are made based on the funding level and administrative/management burden to the Mission. USAID A&O costs cover salaries, benefits, and associated costs of training and field visits for: four full-time PMI staff (one resident advisor, two technical FSNs, one program assistant); partial salaries and benefits for four USPSC staff working on PMI from Health, Population, and Nutrition (HPN) and contracting offices; and partial salaries and benefits for nine FSNs that contribute to the PMI program from HPN office (SBCC, M&E specialist, Commodities and Logistics Manager, Budget/Operations Manager, Administrative Assistant), the Office of Finance Management, and the Executive Office.

   The total budget for PMI full-time staff (3 FSNs, 1 USAID resident advisor) is $1,118,278 (1.6%). The USAID budget for Oversight and Administration includes partial salaries of staff from OAA, OFM, EXO, and the Program Office that support the PMI program is $1,508,697 (2.0%). *($2,626,975)*

2. *CDC staff and administrative costs:* FY 2016 funding will be used to support oversight for PMI malaria activities and technical assistance to the NMEP. Costs include salaries and associated costs for the CDC PMI resident advisor. *($892.000)*

Table 1: Budget Breakdown by Mechanism

President's Malaria Initiative – NIGERIA
Planned Malaria Obligations for FY 2017

Mechanism	Geographic Area	Activity	Budget ($)	%
GHSC-PSM	11 PMI focus states	Procure, deliver, warehouse, and distribute ITNs, mRDTs, ACTs, and SP for IPTp; and implement mass campaigns in Bauchi and Akwa Ibom States	44,537,000	59%
TBD/US PMI for States	9 PMI focus states	Support malaria service delivery, increase diagnostic and treatment capacity of health workers at facility and community level, including private sector (PPMV); improve MIP service delivery particularly IPTp; strengthen HMIS reporting. Includes support to NMEP to strengthen capacity and leadership role. Support implementation of approved OR activities.	16,358,000	22%
TBD/Integrated Health Program	2 PMI focus states	Support malaria service delivery, increase diagnostic and treatment capacity of health workers at facility and community level; improve MIP service delivery particularly IPTp; strengthen HMIS reporting. Implementation through an integrated program	1,617,000	2%
TBD/SBCC	11 PMI focus states	Integrated SBCC activities targeting community level (net use, positive care seeking behavior, ANC attendance), health workers (prompt testing and adherence to test results, IPTp), and state level capacity (SACSM strategy, workplan, implementation and oversight)	5,000,000	7%
TBD/Vector Control	6 PMI focus states	Strengthen entomological monitoring and capacity at federal and state levels.	1,080,000	1%
VectorWorks	3 states	ITN physical integrity monitoring in five monitoring sites	200,000	0%

United States Pharmacopeia	Nationwide	Strengthen NAFDAC capacity for drug quality control including support for Minilabs® for post-market surveillance activities in the field.	1,000,000	1%
WRAIR	11 focus states	Strengthen capacity for malaria diagnosis including QA/QC activities at national and states.	300,000	0%
TBD/DHS Contract	Nationwide	Support Demographic Health Survey in 2018	300,000	0%
MEASURE Evaluation	Nationwide	Strengthen routine health management information at national and state levels	300,000	0%
TBD/Learning Project	Nationwide	Mission-wide M&E services contract and M&E support to Project	220,025	0%
CDC IAA	Nationwide	CDC TDYs to support entomology, IRS, SM&E, and case management activities; support for FELTP for five NMEP personnel. This line also includes CDC annual staffing and administration costs of $630,000.	1,461,000	2%
USAID	Nationwide	Support for USAID annual staffing and administration costs	2,626,975	4%
Total			**75,000,000**	**100%**

Table 2: Budget Breakdown by Activity

President's Malaria Initiative – NIGERIA
Planned Malaria Obligations for FY 2017

Proposed Activity	Mechanism	Budget		Geographic Area	Description
		Total $	Commodity $		
PREVENTIVE ACTIVITIES					
VECTOR MONITORING AND CONTROL					
Entomologic monitoring and insecticide resistance management					
Conduct entomological monitoring at select sentinel sites	TBD/Vector Control	680,000	0	6 Sentinel sites	Provide support for vector surveillance and susceptibility monitoring in 6 sentinel sites across 4 ecological zones in the country. Activity will include vector surveillance activities and insecticidal resistance monitoring.
Strengthen national capacity for entomological surveillance	TBD/Vector Control	350,000	0	Federal and select States	Strengthen capacity for entomological expertise at federal and state levels with training and equipment support. Specific capacities include WHO cone wall bioassay, light trap collections, and others. The activity also includes maintenance of insectary at Keffi- Nasarawa state.

Activity	Implementing Mechanism			Location	Activity Details
Entomological technical assistance	CDC IAA	29,000	0	Federal and select States	Two trips to provide insecticide resistance training for Nigerian NMEP/AIRS staff, resistance test kits, and insecticide for Nigerian vector control officers attending training.
Subtotal Entomological monitoring		1,059,000	0		
Insecticide-treated Nets					
Procurement of ITNs	GHSC-PSM	23,776,480	23,776,480	11 PMI focus states	Procure 8,255,722 ITNs and deliver to state warehouses of which 7,079,567 ITNs are for mass campaigns in Bauchi (3,856,640) and Akwa Ibom (3,222,927); and 1,176,155 ITNs for continuous distribution and IDPs.
Distribution of ITNs from state warehouses to service delivery points	GHSC-PSM	1,000,000	0	11 PMI focus states	Distribute approximately 1 million nets from state ware houses to service delivery points for continuous distribution.
Logistics and operational cost for ITN distribution	GHSC-PSM	6,490,520	0	2 focus states	Distribute 7 million nets through mass campaign in Bauchi and Sokoto States. Costs include technical assistance, training, microplanning, and registration. BCC/Social mobilization costs are reflected separately in the SBCC section.
ITN durability monitoring	VectorWorks	200,000	0	3 states	Continue ITN durability monitoring in 3 monitoring sites.
Subtotal ITNs		31,467,000	23,776,480		
Indoor Residual Spraying					

Activity	Mechanism			Location	Description
Technical assistance to NMEP IRS activities	TBD Vector Control	50,000	0	Nationwide	Provide technical assistance for IRS at federal and states.
Subtotal IRS		50,000	0		
SUBTOTAL VECTOR MONITORING AND CONTROL		**32,576,000**	**23,776,480**		
Malaria in Pregnancy					
Procurement of SP	GHSC- PSM	540,000	540,000	11 PMI focus states	Procure 3 million treatments and deliver SP to state warehouses.
Support to MIP activities	TBD/US PMI for States	1,300,000	0	National and 9 states	Support implementation of MIP and IPTp activities as part of FANC across the nine PMI-supported states. Support will include training, introducing new guidelines in medical training institutions and professional associations, and the job mentoring of health workers and reporting.
Support to MIP activities	TBD/IHP	500,000	0	2 States	Support implementation of MIP and IPTp activities as part of FANC across two PMI-supported states. Support will include training, introducing new guidelines in medical training institutions and professional associations, on the job mentoring of health workers and reporting.
Subtotal Malaria in Pregnancy		2,340,000	540,000		

SUBTOTAL PREVENTIVE		34,916,000	24,316,480		
CASE MANAGEMENT					
Diagnosis and Treatment					
Procurement of RDTs	GHSC- PSM	5,300,000	5,300,000	11 PMI focus states	Procure 16,562,500 million RDTs and deliver to warehouses in 11 states. This will fill gaps and help prevent stockouts of malaria diagnostics tests in the public sector facilities.
Strengthen malaria diagnosis, including QA/QC system	WRAIR	300,000	0	Federal and 11 states	Support implementation for QA for malaria diagnosis. Also support existing lab in one state to act as reference lab for malaria diagnosis QA/QC. Conduct training of trainers as needed for new state and support malaria diagnosis.
Procurement of ACTs	GHSC- PSM	2,580,000	2,580,000	11 PMI focus states	Procure 3 million doses of AL and deliver to warehouse. ACTs will fill gaps and prevent stock out of antimalaria medications in the public sector.
Procure Sulfadoxine/Pyrimethamine +Amodiaquine (SP+AQ) for SMC	GHSC-PSM	850,000	850,000	3 states	Procure 1,689,300 treatments of SP+AQ for SMC in select LGAs in Kebbi, Zamfara, and Sokoto States.

Build capacity, and strengthen service delivery for case management at public health facilities in 9 states of Zamfara, Kebbi, Nasarawa, Oyo, Benue, Ebonyi, Cross River, Akwa Ibom and Plateau	TBD/ US PMI for States	9,965,250	0	9 States	Training of health care workers at all levels on malaria case management in public health facilities. Also include conducting supportive supervision, on-the-job capacity building, and providing basic tools and job aids for malaria case management in public sector.
Build capacity for case management at public health facilities in the two states of Bauchi and Sokoto	TBD/Integrated Health Program	500,000	0	2 states	Training of health care workers at all levels on malaria case management in public health facilities. Also include conducting supportive supervision, on-the-job capacity building, and providing basic tools and job aids for malaria case management in public sector.
Build capacity and scale up malaria case management in the private sector facilities, including PPMVs and iCCM	TBD/ US PMI for States	841,000	0	2 states	Expand malaria case management in private health sector using lessons from the iCCM pilots. Facilities to be targeted include PPMVs and private clinics in up two two southern states.
Therapeutic efficacy studies	TBD/US PMI for States	300,000	0	5 TES sites located in 5 States	Support DTET in five sentinel sites @ $60,000/site to monitor efficacy to first-line antimalarial drugs. This will include the K-13 analysis.

Support implementation of SMC in two states	TBD/ US PMI for States	951,750	0		Implementation of SMC in Kebbi and Zamfara states, including microplanning, training, drug administration, supervision, monitoring, and reporting.
Support implementation of SMC in one state	TBD/Integrated Health Program	317,000	0		Implementation of SMC in Sokoto State, including microplanning, training, drug administration, supervision, monitoring, and reporting.
Technical assistance for case management	CDC IAA	20,000	0	Federal and 11 states	Two CDC TDYs to provide technical support to case management.
Subtotal Diagnosis and Treatment		**21,925,000**	**8,730,000**		
Pharmaceutical Management					
Supply chain strengthening	GHSC PSM	4,000,000	0		Strengthen the pharmaceutical management system, forecasting, management, and distribution of pharmaceuticals and RDTs. Conduct EUVs in PMI-supported states twice a year; Provide warehousing and distribution of PMI procured commodities to the health facilities; including support to data management.

103

Strengthen regulatory authority (NAFDAC) on drug surveillance	USP/PQM	Strengthen NAFDAC's capacity for drug quality control including the procurement of necessary equipment and supplies. Support will include deployment and use of minilabs for field testing of drugs. Activities include post market surveillance in priority states to detect counterfeit and poor quality medicines as well as monotherapies.	1,000,000	0
Subtotal Pharmaceutical Management			**5,000,000**	**0**
SUBTOTAL CASE MANAGEMENT			**26,925,000**	**8,730,000**

HEALTH SYSTEM STRENGTHENING / CAPACITY BUILDING

Strengthen technical capacity of NMEP	TBD/US PMI for States	Support for NMEP's role as lead coordination body through meeting support, monitoring support, and training. Support will include NMCP technical Support will include deployment and use of minilabs for field testing of drugs. Activities include post market surveillance in priority states to detect counterfeit and poor quality medicines as well as monotherapies. to states and LGAs.	500,000	0	National

104

Activity	Mechanism	Location	Amount	Description
Strengthen capacity of states and LGAs for planning and management of malaria services	TBD/US PMI for States	9 states	1,000,000	Support the PMI-supported states to plan, implement, coordinate, and monitor their malaria control programs. Long term TA to support SMEP. The nine states are: Cross River, Zamfara, Nasarawa, Benue, Ebonyi, Oyo, Kogi, Akwa Ibom, and Kebbi. Benue and Sokoto will be supported with Mission MCH funds under the TBD/Health Integrated Program.
Support for NFELTP	CDC IAA	National	500,000	Support training for five fellows for the two-year FELTP course ($50,000/year/trainee). Funds will support 5 new fellows and 5 existing fellows.
SUBTOTAL HSS & CAPACITY BUILDING			**2,000,000**	
SOCIAL AND BEHAVIOR CHANGE COMMUNICATION				
Support to national 'Malaria-free' campaign	TBD/SBCC	National	1,200,000	A National 'malaria–free campaign' will utilize the national malaria song, educational radio, and television drama shows targeted at 20% of population.
Community mobilization and interpersonal communication through community outreach and engagement	TBD/SBCC	11 PMI focus states	1,500,000	Work with community leadership structures and potential champions such as religious and community leaders, civil society organizations, and opinion leaders to reach about 5 million people to mobilize behavior change in communities.

105

Activity	Partner	Amount		Coverage	Description
SBCC for seasonal malaria chemoprevention campaign	TBD/SBCC	300,000	0	3 PMI focus states	SBCC activities will be done to promote sustained adherence to SMC throughout the campaign period.
Communication initiatives to improve RDT trust and use	TBD/SBCC	700,000	0	11 PMI focus states	Using group interactions and health worker engagement to build confidence and trust in malaria diagnostics.
SBCC activities to strengthen health workers compliance with updated IPTp policy	TBD/SBCC	400,000	0	11 PMI focus states	Using multiple channels to strengthen adherence to clinical guidelines and match demand with supply of quality ANC services.
Promote ITN uptake and use during mass distribution campaign in states	TBD/SBCC	600,000	0	3 PMI focus states	Coordinate and implement evidenced SBCC activities in states during mass campaigns.
Support school-based SBCC campaign	TBD/SBCC	300,000	0	7 PMI focus states	Conduct SBCC activities targeted at schoolchildren especially in states with high school attendance rates.
SUBTOTAL SBCC		**5,000,000**	**0**		
SURVEILLANCE, MONITORING, AND EVALUATION					
Strengthen routine SM&E systems at federal level	MEASURE Evaluation	300,000	0	Federal	Strengthen coordination and harmonization of HMIS at the Federal Ministry of Health and NMEP.
Strengthen routine SM&E systems at state level	TBD/US PMI for States	1,500,000	0	9 states	Strengthen the harmonized HMIS at health facility, LGA, and state levels in nine PMI-

Activity	Mechanism	Budget		Coverage	Description
					supported states.
Strengthen routine SM&E at State level	TBD/IHP	300,000	0	2 states	Strengthen the harmonized HMIS at health facility, LGA, and state levels in Bauchi and Sokoto states.
Conduct a national Demographic Health Survey	TBD/DHS Contract	300,000	0	Nationwide	Contribute funding to support the malaria module of the 2018 NDHS.
Mission-wide M&E services contract	USAID/Learning Project	220,025	0	Federal and 11 states	PMI contribution to Mission-wide M&E services. Budget is part of USAID PD&L.
Technical assistance for SM&E strengthening	CDC IAA	20,000	0	Federal and 11 states	Two CDC TDYs to provide technical support for surveillance, monitoring, and evaluation.
SUBTOTAL SM&E		**2,640,025**	**0**		
OPERATIONAL RESEARCH					
		0	0		
SUBTOTAL OR		**0**	**0**		
IN-COUNTRY STAFFING AND ADMINISTRATION					
In-country staffing and administration costs	CDC IAA	892,000	0	Nationwide	Support for annual CDC staffing and administrative costs.

107

In-country staffing and administration costs	USAID	Nationwide	
	2,626,975	0	Support for USAID annual staffing and administration costs. Also includes A&O and PD&L. To include two malaria technical specialists for the PMI program.
SUBTOTAL IN-COUNTRY STAFFING	**3,518,975**	**0**	
GRAND TOTAL	**75,000,000**	**33,046,480**	

www.ingramcontent.com/pod-product-compliance
Lightning Source LLC
Chambersburg PA
CBHW081327310526
45789CB00018B/2474